2700 Quotes

for Sermons

and Addresses

2700 QUOTES

FOR SERMONS

AND ADDRESSES

BAKER BOOK HOUSE
Grand Rapids, Michigan

2700 QUOTES

FOR SERMONS

AND ADDRESSES

Compiled By

E.C. McKENZIE

BAKER BOOK HOUSE
Grand Rapids, Michigan

PHOTOLITHOPRINTED BY CUSHING - MALLOY, INC.
ANN ARBOR, MICHIGAN, UNITED STATES OF AMERICA
1974

CONTENTS

A

Ability 7
Accomplishment . .7
Action 8
Adversity 9
Advice 10
Agreement 11
Aim 11
Ambition 12
Anger 13
Appreciation 14
Arguments 14
Athcists 15
Authority 16

B

Behavior 16
Bible 18
Boasting 20
Brotherhood 20
Burdens 21

C

Caution 21
Character 21
Charity 23
Cheerfulness 23
Children 24
Child Training . . .25
Choice 26
Christianity 26
Christians 27
Christmas 28
Church 29
Church
    Attendance 30
Church Members .31
Common Sense . .32
Complaining 33
Compliments 33
Compromise 34
Conceit 34
Confession 35

Confusion 36
Conscience 36
Contentment 37
Conviction 38
Courage 38
Courtesy 39
Criticism 40
Critics 41
Crookedness 41

D

Dancing 41
Death 42
Decision 43
Deeds 43
Defeat 43
Difficulties 44
Dignity 44
Disappointments .44
Discretion 45
Dissipation 45
Divorce 46
Doubt 47
Drunkards 47
Duty 47

E

Education 48
Egotism 49
Enemies 50
Enthusiasm 51
Envy 51
Error 52
Evil 52
Example 52
Excuses 53
Experience 54

F

Facts 54
Failure 55
Faith 56

Family Trees 57
Faultfinding 57
Faults 57
Flattery 58
Fools 59
Forgiveness 59
Friends 60
Friendship 61
Future 61

G

Gambling 62
Gentlemen 63
Giving 63
God 64
Golden Rule 65
Goodness 66
Gossip 66
Gratitude 67
Grouches 67
Grudges 68
Grumbling 68

H

Habits 68
Happiness 69
Hatred 70
Heaven 70
Home 71
Honesty 72
Hope 73
Humility 73
Hypocrites 74

I

Ideals 74
Ideas 75
Idleness 75
Ignorance 76
Improvement . . .76
Influence 77
Intelligence 77

5

J

Judging 78
Judgement 78
Justice 79
Juvenile
   Delinquency . . . 79

K

Kindness 80
Knocking 81
Knowledge 82

L

Laughter 83
Laziness 83
Leadership 84
Liars 85
Liberty 85
Lies 86
Life 86
Liquor 87
Love 87
Luck 88

M

Man 88
Marriage 89
Memory 90
Mind 90
Mistakes 91
Money 91
Mother 92
Music 92

N

Nature 93
Neighbors 94
New Year 95

O

Old Age 95

Opinions 96
Opportunity 97
Our Needs 97

P

Parents 98
Patience 99
Peace 100
People 101
Perfection 102
Pessimists 102
Popularity 103
Poverty 103
Prayer 104
Preachers 105
Prejudice 106
Problems 106
Prosperity 107

Q

Questions 108

R

Religion 108
Repentance . . . 110
Reputation . . . 110
Responsibility . . 111
Revenge 112
Riches 112
Righteousness . . 113
Right Living . . . 113
Rumors 114

S

Scandals 114
Self-control . . . 115
Selfishness 115
Sermons 116
Silence 117
Sin 118
Success 120

T

Talkativeness . . . 121
Teen-agers 122
Temper 123
Temptation . . . 123
Thinking 124
Thrift 125
Time 126
Tolerance 126
Tongue(the) . . . 127
Trouble 127
Truth 128

U

Unbelief 129
Unity 130

V

Values 130
Vices 131
Virtue 131

W

Wages 131
War 132
Wealth 133
Wild Oats 133
Wisdom 134
Words 135
Work 136
World 136
Worry 137
Worship 139

Y

Youth 139

Z

Zeal 140

A

ABILITY

Many men doubt their ability, but few have any misgivings about their importance.

You can always tell luck from ability by its duration.

We rate ability in men by what they finish, not by what they attempt.

Executive ability is a talent for deciding something quickly and getting somebody else to do it.

It is better to have a little ability and to use it well than to have much ability and make poor use of it.

Be big enough to admit and admire the abilities of people who are better than you are.

What lies behind us and what lies before us are tiny matters compared to what lies within us.

The remarkable thing about most of us is our ability to live beyond our means.

Ability is what will get you to the top if the boss has no daughter.

Executive ability is the art of getting credit for all the hard work that somebody else does.

Ability is the most important tool in your life.

ACCOMPLISHMENT

Some fellows dream of worthy accomplishments while others stay awake and do them.

It is when we forget ourselves that we do things that are most likely to be remembered.

You can't make a place for yourself under the sun if you keep sitting in the shade of the family tree.

It is simply remarkable how the Apostle Paul covered so much territory and accomplished so much without a car.

A man seldom knows what he can do until he tries to undo what he did.

Don't measure yourself by what you have accomplished, but by what you should have accomplished with your ability.

Most of us are inclined to measure our accomplishments by what other people haven't done.

There are four steps to accomplishment: Plan purposefully. Prepare prayerfully. Proceed positively. Pursue persistently.

A man's accomplishment in business depends partly on whether he keeps his mind or his feet on the desk.

ACTION

The actions of men are the best interpreters of their thoughts.

Action speaks louder than words but not nearly as often.

We cannot do everything we want to do, but we can do everything God wants us to do.

Having a great aim in life is important. So is knowing when to pull the trigger.

"Push" will get a person almost everywhere—except through a door marked "pull."

Every action of our lives touches some chord that will vibrate in eternity.

Kind words can never die, but without kind deeds they can sound mighty sick.

People may doubt what you say, but they will always believe what you do.

It is a great deal better to do all the things you should do than to spend the rest of your life wishing you had.

Don't forget that people will judge you by your actions, not your intentions. You may have a heart of gold—but so does a hard-boiled egg.

You can't get anywhere unless you start.

Begin where you are! But don't stay where you are.

It pays to keep your feet on the ground, but keep them moving.

If you're going to climb, you've got to grab the branches, not the blossoms.

It doesn't do any good to sit up and take notice if you keep on sitting.

You can do everything you ought to do.

No one ever climbed a hill just by looking at it.

The fellow who has an abundance of push gets along without a pull.

Don't sit back and take what comes. Go after what you want.

A lot of going concerns are going in the wrong direction.

Actions speak louder than words—and are just as apt to be misquoted or misinterpreted.

A man ordinarily has time to do the things he wants to do.

When you do something and don't want anybody to know it, it's very good or very bad.

Our ship probably would come in much sooner if we'd only swim out to meet it.

Knowing without doing is like plowing without sowing.

The best time to do something worthwhile is between yesterday and tomorrow.

ADVERSITY

In adversity, a man can very well become acquainted with himself because he is free from admirers.

Another thing learned in adversity is that a tire isn't the only thing you can patch.

We learn some things from prosperity, but we learn many more from adversity.

When things get rough, remember: It's the rubbing that brings out the shine.

The average man can stand adversity better than prosperity.

When you're down and out something always turns up—and it's usually the noses of your friends.

Adversity is the only diet that will reduce a fat head.

He who swells in prosperity will shrink in adversity.

Adversity is never pleasant, but sometimes it is possible to learn lessons from it that can be learned in no other way.

The chill winds of adversity usually blows off a lot of high hats.

ADVICE

An intelligent person not only knows how to take advice, but also how to reject it.

Advice is that which the wise don't need and fools won't take.

Medicine and advice are two things more pleasant to give than to receive.

Advice is the only commodity on the market where the supply always exceeds the demand.

We naturally admire the wisdom and good judgment of those who come to us for advice.

The best advice is only as good as the use we make of it.

"Be yourself" is about the worst advice you can give to some people.

Advice is seldom welcome. Those who need it most, like it least.

No one gives out advice with more enthusiasm than an ignorant person.

Free advice is the kind that costs you nothing unless you act upon it.

When you give advice, remember that Socrates was a Greek philosopher who went around giving advice. They poisoned him.

How much easier it is to give advice than to lend a helping hand!

Most of us find it hard to take advice from people who need it more than we do.

The only time to give advice is when it is asked for.

When a man gets too old to set a bad example, he usually starts giving good advice.

We don't mind if someone wants to give us advice; we only object if they insist we take it.

The better the advice, the harder it is to take.

It is as easy to give advice to yourself as to others—and as useless.

Seldom does the one who really needs advice ask for it.

The trouble with giving advice is that people want to repay you.

Advice may be had for nothing and is usually worth it.

Free advice may prove to be the costliest kind.

We give advice but we cannot give the wisdom to profit by it.

When a person starts out handing you a lot of free advice, it's pretty certain it wasn't worth keeping for personal use.

It is advisable to be careful when you give advice—somebody might take it.

It takes a great man to give sound advice tactfully, but a greater man to accept it graciously.

Some people never take advice from anybody, others take advice from everybody.

The best things in life are free; also the worst advice.

Some advice isn't worth the trouble of taking.

Keeping advice to yourself isn't selfish; it's just good public relations.

Advice is like mushrooms—consuming the wrong kind might prove fatal.

Too many people are cheerful givers only when they get a chance to hand out free advice.

Advice to hunters: Do not get loaded when your gun is.

The one thing young people in love don't want is advice.

We might be more eager to accept good advice if it did not continually interfere with our plans.

AGREEMENT

A "gentleman's agreement" is a deal which neither party cares to put in writing.

It is never wise to agree with a fool—the by-standers might not know which is which.

Reasonable men always agree if they understand what they are talking about.

When two men in business always agree, one of them is unnecessary.

It is a pretty safe rule that the fellow who always agrees with you in everything you say is not worth talking to.

We like people who agree with us and food that doesn't.

Usually it's a lot easier to nod as if you agree with someone than it would be to explain why you don't.

AIM

There is a difference between having an aim in life and just shooting at random.

Many people have a good aim in life but they never pull the trigger.

There is no point in trying to carry the ball until you learn where the goal is.

We never see the target a man aims at in life; we see only the target he hits.

Any one can be a sure shot if he aims and shoots first and draws the circle afterwards.

One going nowhere can be sure of reaching his destination.

The greatest danger for most of us is not that our aim is too high and we miss it, but that our aim is too low and we reach it.

You seldom hit anything unless you aim at it.

Many people aim to do right but are just poor shots.

It is useless to have an aim in life unless one has ammunition to back it up.

No man ever drifted into manhood.

Following the line of least resistance is what makes rivers and men crooked.

AMBITION

A man with a burning ambition is seldom fired.

The ambition of most girls is to make some man a good husband.

You can often gauge a man's ambition by whether he hates his alarm clock or considers it his best friend.

The tragedy is that so many have ambition, and so few have ability.

Ambition without determination has no destination.

Watch out for ambition! It can get you into a lot of hard work.

Some young men who leave home to set the world on fire usually have to come back home for more matches.

No power on earth can keep a first class man down or a fourth class man up.

Ambition never gets anywhere until it forms a partnership with work.

The average man's ambition is to be able to afford what he is spending.

Ambition may be the main thing that keeps people moving, but the "No Parking" sign is doing its part.

One of the secret ambitions of many people is to be able to enjoy some of the evils which go with having too much money.

ANGER

Anger is that feeling that makes your mouth work faster than your mind.

There is always a reason for anger—but never a good one.

Had you ever noticed that a fire department never fights fire with fire?

The fellow who gets on a high horse is riding for a fall.

You shouldn't get angry at someone who knows more than you do. After all, it's not his fault.

To be angry with a weak man is proof that you are not very strong yourself.

Anger is only one letter short of danger.

The best way to get rid of a hot-head is to give him the cold shoulder.

People who fly into a rage always make a bad landing.

When angry, count ten before speaking. When very angry, count one hundred and then don't speak.

No matter whether you are on the road or in an argument, when you see red, STOP!

For every minute you are angry, you lose sixty seconds of happiness.

Anger is a wind that blows out the lamp of the mind.

One of the sorriest spectacles imaginable is the anger of two people who have gotten into an argument over something that neither of them know anything about.

The world needs more warm hearts and fewer hot heads.

When you see a married couple coming down the street, the one who is two or three steps ahead is the one that's mad.

Anyone who angers you conquers you.

Every time you give some one a piece of your mind you make your head a little emptier.

Men with clenched fists cannot shake hands.

The emptier the pot, the quicker it boils—watch your temper!

You are not a dynamic person simply because you blow your top.

No one can be reasonable and angry at the same time.

Be strong enough to control your anger instead of letting it control you.

Striking while the iron is hot is all right, but don't strike while the head is hot.

The man who cannot be angry at evil usually lacks enthusiasm for good.

13

APPRECIATION

Appreciation is what some people lack when you do them a favor.

The world's most unsatisfied hunger is hunger for appreciation.

It is better to appreciate something you cannot have than to have something you cannot appreciate.

You must speak up to be heard, but sometimes you have to shut up to be appreciated.

Some wives appreciate their husbands the most while they are away at work.

Appreciation makes people feel more important than most anything you can give them.

ARGUMENTS

Sometimes when you are arguing with a fool, he is doing the same thing.

An argument usually produces plenty of heat, but no light.

The more arguments you win, the fewer friends you'll have.

It is impossible to defeat an ignorant man in an argument.

The less a thing can be proved, the angrier we get when we argue about it.

An argument is where two people are trying to get in the last word first.

Many an argument is sound—and only sound.

In an argument, the best weapon to hold is your tongue.

The surest sign that you have no brains is to argue with one who hasn't.

Some people are so argumentative they won't even eat food that agrees with them.

The weaker the argument, the stronger the words.

You get out of an argument exactly what you put into it—a lot of hot air.

Discussion is an exchange of knowledge; argument is only an exchange of ignorance.

The only people who listen to both sides of a family argument are those who live next door.

An argument is a question with two sides—and no end.

Men who know the least always argue the most.

It is never wise to argue with a fool—the listeners might not know which is which.

There are a lot of hot arguments over cold cash.

It is a rare thing to win an argument and the other fellow's respect at the same time.

An argument is a collision between two trains of thought in which both are derailed.

If it is fair to hear both sides of an argument, it is heavenly to hear the end of it.

Never argue with a woman. You might win—and then you're really in trouble.

If you must argue, the best way to win is to start by being right.

Most of us are broad-minded; in an argument we see both points of view, the one that is wrong and our own.

ATHEISTS

The worst moment in the life of an atheist is when he really is thankful and has nobody to thank.

An atheist hopes the Lord will do nothing to disturb his disbelief.

The atheist cannot find God for the same reason that a thief cannot find a policeman.

Some flatter themselves that they are atheists, when in reality they are only heathen.

An atheist is a disbeliever who prefers to raise his children in a Christian community.

A good question for an atheist is to serve him a fine meal and then ask him if he believes there is a cook.

All atheists pray at times when they can find no other way out of their troubles.

An atheist is the fellow who shakes his fist and defies the God he claims doesn't exist.

AUTHORITY

Give some people authority and they grow, give it to others and they swell.

Nothing intoxicates some people like a sip of authority.

There is just as much authority in the family today as there ever was—only now the children exercise it.

Nothing pleases a little man more than an opportunity to crack a big whip.

If there's anything small, or shallow, or ugly about a person, giving him a little authority will bring it out.

B

BEHAVIOR

A lot of good behavior is due to poor health.

To really know a man, observe his behavior with a woman, a flat tire, and a child.

It's nice to be important, but it is more important to be nice.

No matter what you do, someone always knew you would.

A father is usually more pleased to have his child look like him than act like him.

Some folks sow wild oats during the week and then go to church on Sunday and pray for a crop failure.

No man is as important as he sounds at his alumni banquet.

Always hold your head up but be careful to keep your nose at a friendly level.

The sure way to gain respect is to earn it by conduct.

You can't hold another fellow down in the ditch unless you stay down there with him.

Most of us don't put our best foot forward until we get the other one in hot water.

Some people never say anything bad about the dead, or anything good about the living.

Wouldn't it be wonderful if everybody behaved as he thinks the other fellow ought to behave?

When little Junior acts cute, he deserves to get a big hand—in the right place.

Judging from the way some people behave these days, they must think that hell has been air-conditioned.

When in Rome do as the Romans do, if the Romans do as they ought to do.

The kind of behavior that once brought shame and disgrace now brings a book, movie, and a television contract.

No man has a right to do as he pleases, except when he pleases to do right.

Actually there's only a slight difference between keeping your chin up and sticking your neck out, but it's worth knowing.

We count our blessings on our fingers and our miseries on an adding machine.

There are no detour signs along the straight and narrow path.

Think what others ought to be like, then start being like that yourself.

It may be bad to talk when your mouth is full, but it isn't too good either when your head is empty.

What a scarcity of news there would be if everybody obeyed the Ten Commandments.

When men speak evil of you, so live that no one will believe them.

The behavior of some children suggests that their parents embarked on the sea of matrimony without a paddle.

Don't be a carbon copy of something. Make your own impressions.

It's easy to save face. Just keep the lower half of it tightly closed.

Blowing out the other fellow's candle won't make yours shine any brighter.

By the time most folks learn to behave themselves, they are too old to do anything else.

Good behavior gets a lot of credit that really belongs to a lack of opportunity.

No one can stay young very long, but some manage to act like children all their lives.

Men and nations do behave wisely—once all other alternatives have been exhausted.

We try to see some good in everybody we meet, but occasionally there are some folks who make us realize our eyesight isn't as good as it once was.

Anybody whose behavior is normal these days is probably eccentric.

BIBLE

Dust on your Bible is not evidence that it is a dry book.

It is impossible to mentally and socially enslave a Bible reading people.

Men do not usually reject the Bible because it contradicts itself, but because it contradicts them.

Some people thank God for the open Bible who never bother to open it.

The Bible promises no loaves to the loafer.

Take all the Bible you can on reason and the rest by faith.

One of the best evidences of the inspiration and infallibility of the Bible is that it has survived the fanaticism of its friends.

The most desirable time to read the Bible is as often as possible.

It is an awful responsibility to own a Bible.

Bible verses will save you from spiritual reverses.

A Bible stored in the mind is worth a dozen stored in the bottom of one's trunk.

We should read the Bible as a privilege, not as a duty.

Study the Bible to be wise; believe it to be safe; practice it to be holy.

Other books have been given to us for information, but the Bible was given to us for transformation.

If all the neglected Bibles in this country were dusted off at the same time, we would suffer the worst dust storm we have experienced in many years.

No one is saved by buying a Bible he does not read, nor is one saved by reading a Bible he does not obey.

The Gideons should send a Bible to those hotel authorities who determine the room rates.

Those who don't read the Bible have no advantage over those who can't read it.

There's a big difference between the books that men make and the Book that makes men.

How can you have faith in the Bible unless you know what is in it?

The Bible contains the vitamins of soul health.

A thumb print on the Bible is more important than a footprint on the moon.

The Bible finds us where we are, and if permitted, takes us where we ought to go.

A book which will lift men up to God must have come down from God.

The Bible is rejected by the world and neglected by the church. How can Christians expect the world to respect a book they neglect?

You can't understand all you read in the Bible, but you can obey what you do understand.

The way some people use the Sword of the Spirit, one would think it was made for splitting hairs.

God does not open the window of heaven to the person who keeps his Bible shut.

The devil can quote Scripture for his purpose.

Our forefathers built this country with three tools: An ax, a plow, and a book. That book was the Bible.

The Bible is not only the world's best seller; it is man's best purchase.

Don't criticize the Bible; let the Bible criticize you.

One evidence of the value of the Bible is the character of those who oppose it.

If you will carry the Bible while you are young, it will carry you when you are old.

A person who merely samples the word of God occasionally never acquires much of a taste for it.

The Bible has survived the ignorance of its friends and the hatred of its enemies.

If the Bible is mistaken in telling us from whence we came, how can we trust it to tell us where we are going?

The Bible has nothing to fear—except neglect.

Carrying your Bible will never take the place of reading it.

Satan is not afraid of a Bible with dust on it.

A Bible in the hand is worth two in the bookcase.

Read your Bible. A chapter a day keeps Satan away.

BOASTING

The fellow who boasts of his open mind may only have it vacant.

Fellows who boast of being self-made men usually have a few parts missing.

To be important, you must brag either about the extent of your knowledge, or the lack of it.

The hen who laid the biggest egg usually does the least cackling about it.

It is good to be able to boast of our standard of living; but we should also be able to boast of our standard of values.

The fellow who is interested in blowing his horn is seldom interested in harmony.

A boaster and a liar are first cousins.

Few people boast of having been born in log cabins who still live in them.

The man who never boasts is always bragging about it.

Some people would much rather blow their own horn than to listen to the Marine Band.

The man who has a right to boast doesn't have to.

Before you start tooting your own horn be sure there's plenty of juice in your battery.

The man who boasts that he never made a mistake has a wife who did.

Men who boast of running things at home, most likely means the lawn mower, washing machine, vacuum cleaner, and errands.

BROTHERHOOD

The brotherhood of man depends on the manhood of brothers.

We must learn to live together as brothers or we will perish together like fools.

BURDENS

Life's heaviest burden is to have nothing to carry.

Let us not pray for lighter burdens but for stronger backs.

Bearing one another's burdens is very different from bearing down on them.

It's not the load that breaks you down; it's the way you carry it.

Better complain occasionally and carry your burdens than cheerfully push them off on someone else.

There will always be enough for today without taking on yesterday and tomorrow's burdens.

The hardest burdens in life to bear are the things that might happen but usually don't.

A burden must be carried before we can put it down.

The burdens that appear easiest to carry are those borne by others.

C

CAUTION

Caution is one automobile accessory you can't buy.

It is well for the girl with a future to avoid the man with a past.

Watch your step! Everyone else does.

Caution is what we call cowardice in others.

It's all right to be cautious—but even a turtle never gets anywhere until he sticks his neck out.

A man never knows how careful he can be until he gets a new car or wears white shoes.

CHARACTER

Character is easier kept than recovered.

You can buy ready-made clothes, but you can't buy ready-made character.

Think right; act right; it is what you think and do that makes you what you are.

To remove stains from a man's character, let him strike oil suddenly.

Take care of your character and your reputation will take care of itself.

Character is not made in a crisis—it is only exhibited.

Men of genius are admired; men of wealth are envied; men of power are feared; but only men of character are trusted.

It's what you do when you have nothing to do that reveals what you are.

Pay attention to what a man is, not to what he has been.

You can often tell a man's character by what he turns up when offered a job—it's either his nose or his sleeves.

To change one's character, we must begin at the control center—the heart.

Character is made by many acts; it may be lost by a single act.

There is a vast difference between having character and being a character.

A person is never what he ought to be until he is doing what he ought to be doing.

Reputation is what you need to get a job; character is what you need to keep it.

Much may be known of a man's character by what excites his laughter.

Character cannot be purchased, bargained for, inherited, rented, or imported from afar. It must be home-grown.

A good past is the best thing a man can use for a future reference.

Your character is what you have left when you've lost everything you can lose.

There is nothing truly great in man but character.

The measure of a man's character is what he would do if he knew he would never be found out.

You can't give character to another person, but you can encourage him to develop one by possessing one yourself.

There are two very difficult things in the world. One is to make a good name for oneself, and the other is to keep it.

Only you can damage your character.

Character is the one thing we make in this world and take with us into the next.

How a man plays the game shows something of his character. How he loses shows all of it.

Character does not reach its best until it is controlled, harnessed and disciplined.

The measure of a man's character is not what he gets from his ancestors, but by what he leaves his descendants.

Character grows in the soil of experience, with the fertilization of example, the moisture of desire, and the sunshine of satisfaction.

A man's character and his garden both reflect the amount of weeding that was done during the growing season.

CHARITY

Charity is the sterilized milk of human kindness.

In the old days charity was a virtue instead of an industry.

Charity should begin at home, but most people don't stay at home long enough to begin it.

It is better to give than to lend, and it costs about the same.

Unless a man is a recipient of charity, he should be a contributor to it.

Charity is often injurious unless it helps the recipient to become independent of it.

Charity is a virtue of the heart and not the hand.

Real charity doesn't care if it's deductible or not.

Christian charity knows no iron curtain.

Charity is twice blessed—it blesses him who gives and him who receives.

Giving advice to the poor is about as near charity as some people ever get.

Charity often consists of a generous impulse to give away something we have no further use for.

True charity simply means helping those you have every reason to believe would not help you.

CHEERFULNESS

Keep your face to the sunshine and you will never see the shadows.

Remember the steam kettle! Though up to its neck in hot water, it continues to sing.

Few cases of eye strain have been developed by looking on the bright side of things.

Your day goes the way the corners of your mouth turn.

Lots of people get credit for being cheerful when they are just proud of their teeth.

Cheerfulness greases the axles of the world.

Some people are able to spread cheer wherever they don't go.

Cheerfulness is contagious, but don't wait to catch it from others. Be a carrier.

The man who gets along in the world is the one who can look cheerful and happy when he isn't.

CHILDREN

Children may tear up a house, but they never break up a home.

In the old days, a father didn't have to take his kid to a psychiatrist to find out that he was a little stinker.

Some children are running everything around the house except errands.

A lot of child welfare can be done with a small leather strap.

The one thing that children can wear out faster than shoes is parents.

Infant prodigies are young people with highly imaginative parents.

There are no illegitimate children—only illegitimate parents.

Maybe children could keep in the straight and narrow path better if they could get information from someone who's been over the route.

Children are natural mimics; they act like their parents in spite of every effort to teach them good manners.

It now costs more to amuse a child than it once did to educate his father.

One reason so many children are seen on the streets at night is they're afraid to stay at home alone.

Children need strength to lean on, a shoulder to cry on, and an example to learn from.

There are many "bright children" who should be applauded with one hand.

A baby may not be able to lift very much, but it can hold a marriage together.

Children will be children—even after they are fifty years old.

If brushing up on manners doesn't help some children, the brush should be moved down.

There are still a few people who can remember when a child misbehaved to get attention—got it.

If some children are as bright as their parents think they are, they should be looked at through sunglasses.

The trouble with your children is that when they're not being a lump in your throat, they're being a pain in the neck.

One of the first things that one notices in a backward country is that children are still obeying their parents.

The best time to put the children to bed is when you can.

No two children are alike—particularly if one is yours and the other one isn't.

Children are a great deal more apt to follow your lead than the way you point.

Babies are angels whose wings grow shorter as their legs grow longer.

Nothing seems to make children more affectionate than sticky hands.

It is more important to know where your children are tonight than where your ancestors were when the Mayflower landed.

A wayward child is sometimes straightened out by being bent over.

Children are basically good but are made bad by adults who mishandle them.

When parents cannot control their children in the home, it is extremely difficult for the government to control them on the streets.

Children brought up in Sunday School are seldom brought up in court.

CHILD TRAINING

Theories on how to rear children usually end with the birth of a second child.

It is extremely difficult to train up a boy in the way his father does not go.

A child is better un-born than un-trained.

If a child annoys you, quiet him by brushing his hair—if this doesn't work, use the other side of the brush on the other end of the child.

Every child has a right to be well fed and well led.

To train children at home, it's necessary for both the children and the parents to spend some time there.

Children would be brought up perfectly if families would swap kids. Everybody knows what ought to be done with the neighbor's kids.

The surest way to make it hard for your children is to make it soft for them.

You train a child only until age ten; after that you only influence him.

The child that does not hear about religion at his mother's knee is not likely to hear about it at any other joint.

If you want your child to travel the right road, you must go that way yourself.

Train your child in the way you now know you should have gone yourself.

The best way to bring up children is never to let them down.

More attention to the high chair will put cobwebs on the electric chair.

The secret of bringing up a child properly is in knowing WHEN to give it a big hand—and WHERE!

One trouble with mothers who raise their children by the book is they often use comic books.

Better to teach children the roots of labor than hand them the fruits of yours.

Training children to count is not as important as teaching them WHAT counts.

CHOICE

Choice, not chance, determines destiny.

When you have to make a choice and don't make it; that in itself is a choice.

It is hard to choose between a dainty saint and a dirty sinner.

Few people make a deliberate choice between good and evil—the choice is between what we want to do and what we ought to do.

The choice is simple—you can either stand up and be counted, or lie down and be counted out.

CHRISTIANITY

One of the best things about Christianity is that it must function or fizzle.

If your Christianity won't work where you are, it won't work anywhere.

An empty tomb proves Christianity, an empty church denies it.

If you want to defend Christianity, practice it.

The better we understand Christianity, the less satisfied we are with our practice of it.

Christianity is a way of walking as well as a way of talking.

It is not by accident that the symbol of Christianity is the Cross rather than a featherbed.

Christianity, like sin and taxes, is here to stay.

The true expression of Christianity is not a sigh, but a song.

Christianity is a roll-up-your-sleeves religion.

Those who say they believe in Christianity, and those who practice it are not always the same people.

Christianity has been studied and practiced for ages, but it has been studied far more than it has been practiced.

If you want to convince others of the value of Christianity—live it!

Christianity requires that participants come out of the grandstands and on to the playing fields.

CHRISTIANS

A Christian must carry something heavier on his shoulders than chips.

Some Christians who should be wielding the sword of the Spirit are still tugging at the nursery bottle.

The Cross is easier to the Christian who takes it up than to him who drags it along.

It doesn't take much of a man to be a Christian, but it takes all there is.

A Christian is like ripening corn; the riper he grows the more lowly he bends his head.

Every Christian occupies some kind of a pulpit and preaches some kind of a sermon every day.

Christians are like pianos—grand, square, upright, and no good unless in tune.

A Christian has not lost the power to sin, but the desire to sin.

No one can become a Christian on his own terms.

Happier faces are seen on bottles of iodine than on some Christians.

There may be many Christians who haven't stored up enough treasures to make a down payment on a harp.

It's a little difficult to reconcile the creed of some Christians with their greed.

A real Christian is a person who is as horrified by his own sins as he is by his neighbor's.

A few Christians give the impression they have been baptized in vinegar.

Jesus went about doing good. Many of His followers are content merely to go about.

Christians may not see eye to eye, but they can walk arm in arm.

There is nothing quite as drab as an ex-Christian.

A Christian is a mind through which Christ thinks, a heart through which Christ loves, a voice through which Christ speaks, a hand through which Christ helps.

Christians are not only the salt of the earth but are sugar, too.

Satan is never too busy to rock the cradle of a sleeping Christian.

Too many Christian soldiers fraternize with the enemy.

When Christians feel safe and comfortable, the church is in its greatest danger.

Beware of being a musty, dusty, crusty Christian.

No Christian is strong enough to carry a cross and a prejudice at the same time.

The Christian should learn two things about his tongue—how to hold it and how to use it.

If you were arrested for being a Christian, would there be enough evidence to convict you?

Christians are the light of the world, but the switch must be turned on.

Beware of Christians with an open mouth and a closed pocketbook.

A Christian needs no halo about his head, but he should have a solo in his heart.

Some Christians are like kittens—contented when petted.

CHRISTMAS

He who has no Christmas in his heart will never find Christmas under a tree.

The WAY you spend Christmas is far more important than HOW MUCH.

Keeping Christmas is good, but sharing it is a great deal better.

Christmas is a time for exchanging a lot of things you can't afford for a lot of things you don't want.

The Christmas spirit that goes out with the dried-up Christmas tree is just as worthless.

The best Christmas gift of all is the presence of a happy family all wrapped up with one another.

Christmas is really not a date. It is a state of mind.

Let's have an old-fashioned Christmas this year, but not the kind that comes in bottles.

Christmas is a time when a lot of others besides Santa find themselves in the red.

It's a soul-stirring experience to hear Yule carolers standing in the smog singing, "It came upon a Midnight Clear."

Christmas comes but once a year—and that's enough.

Family ties are stronger at Christmas—louder, too!

CHURCH

A cold church is like cold butter—never spreads very well.

In any church, those who complain the most usually do the least work.

A church that is not reaching out is passing out.

The collection is a church function in which many people take only a passing interest.

The church cannot afford the luxury of loafing.

Too many churches have become distribution points for religious aspirin.

If you want to hear all about the troubles in the church, ask someone who hasn't been there for several months.

We are sometimes so interested in creating the machinery of the church that we let the fire go out in the boiler.

The most expensive piece of furniture in the church is the empty pew.

It is easy to lose interest in the church if you have never made an investment.

The business of the church is to get rid of evil, not to supervise it.

What the church needs today is more calloused hands and fewer calloused hearts.

The best remedy for a sick church is to put it on a missionary diet.

Every church has all the success it prays for and pays for.

The church is a building and loan association to help you build a mansion in heaven.

If the church neglects the children, it is certain that the children will someday neglect the church.

The church offers you something you just can't get elsewhere.

If the church were perfect, you could not belong.

Many churches are now serving coffee after the sermon. Presumably this is to get the people thoroughly awake before they drive home.

When the churches discover they can't successfully compete with the theater, perhaps they will try religion again.

Every church has three classes of members: The workers, the jerkers, and the shirkers.

When the church ceases to be in touch with another world, she is no longer in touch with this world.

The less religion a church has, the more ice cream and cake it takes to keep it going.

A church that is always "chewing the rag" isn't well fed.

The man who says he is just as good as half the folks in the church seldom specifies which half.

Notice in a church bulletin, "The Lord loveth a cheerful giver. He also accepteth from a grouch."

The church service is not a convention to which a family should merely send a delegate.

You need the church, the church needs you, the world needs both.

All churches grow old; but some never grow up.

The church is fairly well equipped with conductors. It shows a shortage of engineers, but an over-plus of brakemen.

CHURCH ATTENDANCE

Church attendance is determined more by desire than by distance.

Some folk's church going is like ice cream—it disappears when the weather gets hot.

A lot of people these days go to prayer meeting to get away from the crowd.

If absence makes the heart grow fonder, some church members are deeply in love with the church.

The automobile does not take people away from the church against their will.

A man's attending church regularly doesn't necessarily mean he attends religiously.

Your absence from church is a vote to close its doors.

Some are late for church service because they have to change a tire; others, because they have to change a dollar.

Perhaps you had never thought of going to church as a beauty treatment, but it is a wonderful way to keep your faith lifted.

Some people go to church to see who didn't.

Too many men who like to talk of finding God in nature rather than in church go hunting for Him with rod and gun.

Depressions, funerals, weddings, and covered-dish suppers keep most people attending church regularly.

Bad weather is a lot like your wife's ill health. It doesn't take much of it to keep you away from church.

Judging by church attendance, heaven won't be crowded with men.

Many people who demand a front seat in a night club try to even things up by taking a back seat in church.

Every person ought to go to church to get away from himself.

CHURCH MEMBERS

A mule can't kick and pull at the same time; neither can a church member.

Some church members are like wheelbarrows: They go only when they are pushed.

If a church member expects to answer when the roll is called up yonder, he had better be present when the roll is called down here.

There are four classes of church members: The tired, the retired, the tiresome and the tireless.

Floating church members make a sinking church.

A lot of church members know the Twenty-third Psalm much better than they know the Shepherd.

31

A sickly saint is likely to be a healthy hypocrite.

Some church members who say, "Our Father," on Sunday go around the rest of the week acting like orphans.

There are still a few church members who are somewhat like the farmer's pond—dried up in the summer and frozen up in the winter.

It is far better to be a weak church member than a strong sinner.

It seems that some church members have been starched and ironed, but too few have been washed.

When a church member rests, he rusts.

"Not good if detached" is true of church members as well as railroad tickets.

There are two kinds of people in your church: Those who agree with you and the bigots.

Church members are stockholders in the church, not spectators.

Most churches have three kinds of members: Pickers, kickers, and stickers.

Judging by the way some church members live, they need fire insurance.

A church member who is immersed in business all week needs to come up for a breath of fresh air on Sunday.

The undertaker is the only one who ought to take names off the church roll.

Hate and bigotry are worse epidemics than the Asian Flu ever was, but there is plenty of vaccine available—at church service every Sunday.

Church membership does not make one a Christian any more than owning a piano makes one a musician.

Church membership is at an all-time high; so is political and social corruption.

COMMON SENSE

Common sense, if applied, would prevent a great many divorces; but, on the other hand, it would also prevent a great many marriages.

An unusual amount of common sense is sometimes called wisdom.

Common sense is something you want the other fellow to show by accepting your ideas and conclusions.

One pound of learning requires ten pounds of common sense to apply it.

It is a thousand times better to have common sense without an education than to have education without common sense.

Common sense is the sixth sense, given by the Creator to keep the other five from making fools of themselves—and us.

Some time during the course of every day, every person ought to make at least a few sensible remarks.

Nowadays, most everybody has everything in common—except common sense.

Emotion and feeling make the world go round, but common sense and reason keep it from going too fast.

Most people have good common sense, but many of them use it only in an emergency or as a last resort.

COMPLAINING

Some of these old codgers who keep complaining that things are not what they used to be always forget to include themselves.

Those who complain about the way the ball bounces are often the ones who dropped it.

The poor complain about the money they can't get, and the rich complain about the money they can't keep.

Don't complain. Every time the lamb bleats he loses a mouthful of hay.

Some people complain because God puts thorns on roses, while others praise Him for putting roses among the thorns.

A lot of people go through life standing at the complaint counter.

It is usually not so much the greatness of our troubles as the littleness of our spirit which makes people complain.

We may complain about the heat in the summer, but at least we don't have to shovel it.

Some people who had no shoes have been known to complain until they met someone who had no feet.

Do not pray for rain if you're going to complain of mud.

COMPLIMENTS

Compliments are like perfume; to be inhaled, not swallowed.

Some pay a compliment as if they expected a receipt.

Everybody knows how to register a complaint, but few can offer a graceful compliment. It takes practice.

A compliment is something which you say to another and which both of you know isn't true.

Be sincere with your compliments. Most people can tell the difference between sugar and saccharine.

It is all right to be always looking for compliments—to give to somebody else.

It's ironic, but the toughest thing to take gracefully is a compliment.

A hammer sometimes misses its mark—a bouquet, never.

Nobody has ever been bored by someone paying them a compliment.

No person is so poor that he cannot give a compliment.

There's a difference between paying compliments and paying FOR them.

A compliment is the soft soap that wipes out a dirty look.

COMPROMISE

A compromise is a deal in which two people get what neither of them wanted.

Compromise is always wrong when it means to sacrifice a principle.

A compromise is the art of dividing a cake in such a way that everyone believes that he got the biggest piece.

Many things are worse than defeat, and compromise with evil is one of them.

CONCEIT

Nature abhors a vacuum. When a head lacks brains, nature fills it with conceit.

Conceit is the only disease known to man that makes everybody sick except the one who has it.

The best remedy for conceit is to sit down and make a list of all the things you don't know.

A conceited man knows a good thing when he sees himself in the mirror.

Heads that are filled with knowledge and wisdom have little space left for conceit.

If you think you are important, just remember that a lot of famous men of a century ago have weeds growing on their graves today.

The world's most conceited man was the fellow who celebrated his birthday by sending his mother a telegram of congratulations.

Conceit may puff a man up, but never props him up.

Conceit is a form of "I" strain that doctors can't cure.

A big shot may also be a big bore.

The person who is all wrapped up in himself is over-dressed.

Talk to a man about himself and he will listen for hours.

Occasionally you meet a person who thinks he is all seven wonders of the world.

The person who sings his own praises is quite likely to be a soloist.

A certain young fellow was so conceited he joined the Navy so the world could see him.

One thing that's hard to keep under your hat is a big head.

Conceit is what makes a little squirt think that he is a fountain of knowledge.

The only time you should blow your horn is when you are in the band.

A conceited person never gets anywhere because he thinks he is already there.

The most conceited person is one whose opinions differ from your own.

CONFESSION

An open confession is good for the soul, but bad for the reputation.

When a woman talks about her past, she's confessing; when a man does, he's boasting.

Confess your sins to the Lord, and you will be forgiven; confess them to men, and you will be laughed at.

An honest confession is not always good for the soul, but in most cases it's cheaper than hiring a high-powered lawyer.

Confessing your sins is no substitute for forsaking them.

CONFUSION

The only thing that isn't hard to get these days is confused.

Most people have plenty of speed, but they don't know what direction they are going.

With the world in such a confused state, no wonder babies cry when they come into it.

A wise man is never confused by what he can't understand, but a fool is sure to be.

When lost, it is better to stand still than to run in the wrong direction. This applies to governments as well as individuals.

Even if this is the dawn of a bright new world, most of us still are in the dark.

No one is more confusing than the fellow who gives good advice while setting a bad example.

If this world becomes any more confused than it is now, don't be surprised to see monkeys tossing peanuts to people.

Some folks think they are busy when they are only confused.

All the world is a stage, and everybody is in a wild scramble trying to get on it.

CONSCIENCE

The modern conscience is made with a lever to throw it out of gear.

As long as your conscience is your friend, never mind about your enemies.

Conscience is that thing that hurts when everything else feels good.

An evil conscience cannot be cured by medicine.

Some people become hard of hearing whenever conscience speaks.

Conscience is that still small voice that often makes you feel smaller.

Quite often when a man thinks his mind is getting broader it is only his conscience stretching.

When you have a fight with your conscience and get licked, you win.

Conscience is that sixth sense that comes to our aid when we are doing wrong and tells us we are about to get caught.

Your conscience doesn't really keep you from doing anything; it merely keeps you from enjoying it.

Many people have succeeded in training their conscience to roll over and play dead.

The testimony of a good conscience is worth more than a dozen character witnesses.

Happy is the man who renounces anything that places a strain upon his conscience.

Nobody's conscience ever kept him awake at night for having exaggerated the good qualities of his friends.

Conscience does not get its guidance from a Gallup poll.

Most people follow their conscience as a man follows a wheelbarrow— pushing it along before him the way he wants it to go.

There is a spark of conscience in each of us, but most of us don't clean our spark plugs often enough.

Conscience is the only mirror that does not flatter.

The best tranquilizer is a good conscience.

Sometimes a man with a clear conscience only has a poor memory.

Your conscience is something like a watch. You trust it, but every so often you ought to check it.

No one works his conscience so hard that it needs a vacation.

It's a pretty good idea to keep on good terms with everybody, but especially with your wife, your banker, your stomach, and your conscience.

CONTENTMENT

It is right to be content with what you have, never with what you are.

Enough is that which would make us content if the neighbors did not have more.

Contentment has been praised more and practiced less than any other condition of life.

The greatest wealth is contentment with a little.

Some folks aren't content with the milk of human kindness—they want the cream.

Contentment is something that depends a little on position and a lot on disposition.

When you can think of yesterday without regret and tomorrow without fear, you are near real contentment.

The best way for a person to have a contented state of mind is for him to count his blessings, not his cash.

Contentment is a matter of hoping for the best and making the best of what you get.

If you would be content, do what you ought, not what you please.

Contentment in life consists not in great wealth, but in simple wants.

When we cannot find contentment in ourselves, it is useless to seek it elsewhere.

The difference between a contented cow and a discontented man is that the cow is still able to produce.

It's difficult to be content if you don't have enough, and it's impossible if you have too much.

CONVICTION

If there is anything stronger than your convictions, it is the heat of your prejudices.

People generally have too many opinions and not enough convictions.

At the age of fifty, one settles down into certain well-defined convictions—most of which are wrong.

A conviction is that commendable quality in ourselves that we call bullheadedness in others.

It is important that people know what you stand for; it is equally important that they know what you won't stand for.

What some people call a conviction may be just a prejudice.

Conviction is a belief that you hold or that holds you.

If you don't stand for something, you will likely fall for anything.

The difference between a prejudice and a conviction is that you can explain a conviction without getting mad.

COURAGE

Be bold in what you stand for but careful in what you fall for.

Have courage to let go the things not worth sticking to.

To ignore an insult is the true test of moral courage.

Too many people consider themselves daring when they are only delirious.

Courage is the quality it takes to look at yourself with candor, your adversaries with kindness, and your setbacks with serenity.

Remember, you are your own doctor when it comes to curing cold feet.

Courage is not the absence of fear, but the conquest of it.

Unfortunately courage is all too often composed of equal parts of bourbon and water.

The test of courage is to be in the minority; the test of tolerance is to be in the majority.

Courage is what it takes to stand up and speak, it is also what it takes, on occasion, to sit and listen.

We must constantly build dikes of courage to hold back the flood of fear.

Courage is something you always have until you need it.

COURTESY

A man once gave a woman his seat on the bus. She fainted. When she revived, she thanked him. Then he fainted.

They say courtesy is contagious; so, why not try to start an epidemic?

Courtesy costs nothing, yet it buys things that are priceless.

Be nice and courteous to people on your way up because you'll meet many of them on your way down.

There is no law against being courteous, even when you are not a candidate for some office.

Practice courtesy. You never know when it might become popular again.

A little of the oil of courtesy will save a lot of friction.

A little courtesy goes a long way—which is understandably due to a shortage.

Courtesy is that quality that keeps a woman smiling when a departing guest stands at the open door and lets the flies in.

It is getting harder and harder to find a courteous person who isn't trying to sell you something.

Courtesy is a form of consideration for others practiced by civilized people when they have the time.

CRITICISM

No need of criticizing yourself, others will be glad to do that for you.

You can always tell a failure by the way he criticizes success.

.Don't criticize the other fellow's plans unless you have better ones to offer.

Criticism is the disapproval of people, not for having faults, but for having faults different from your own.

The difference between coaching and criticism is your attitude.

Small minds are the first to condemn large ideas.

It's a pity that some folks never learn that uncovering the other fellow's faults will never cover up his own.

The trouble with most of us is that we would rather be ruined by praise than saved by criticism.

Stones and sticks are thrown only at fruit-bearing trees.

Those who can—do. Those who can't—criticize.

Any fool can criticize, condemn and complain—and most fools do.

If your head sticks up above the crowd, expect more criticism than bouquets.

When the other fellow picks a flaw in almost everything, he's cranky; when you do, you're discriminating.

Throwing mud at a good man only soils your own hands.

The best place to criticize is in front of your own mirror.

A great many people have the mistaken idea that they can make themselves great by showing how small some one else is.

Don't mind criticism. If it's untrue, disregard it; if it is unfair, keep from irritation; if it is ignorant, smile; if it is justified, learn from it.

A person usually criticizes the individual whom he secretly envies.

Criticism is one thing most of us think is more blessed to give than to receive.

Don't criticize anyone for wishing for what he doesn't have. What else could he wish for?

No one so thoroughly appreciates the value of constructive criticism as the one who's giving it.

Criticizing another's garden does not keep the weeds out of your own.

Before you criticize a person, walk in his shoes awhile.

Criticism should always leave a person with the feeling he has been helped.

CRITICS

How often have you met a critic of the church who tried to make it better?

A critic is one who would have you write it, sing it, play it, or paint it as he would do—if he could.

If it were not for the doers, the critics would soon be out of business.

There's only one way to handle the ignorant or a malicious critic. Ignore him. Everybody else does.

A critic is one who finds fault without a search warrant.

The critic who begins with himself will be too busy to take on outside contracts.

A literary critic is a person who finds meaning in literature that the author didn't know was there.

CROOKEDNESS

The framers of our Constitution aren't its only framers.

A crooked path is the shortest way to the penitentiary.

Following the line of least resistance is what makes rivers and men crooked.

America was in better condition when there were more whittlers and fewer chiselers.

If a man defrauds you one time, he's a rascal; if he does it twice, you're a fool.

D

DANCING

The difference between wrestling and dancing is that some holds are barred in wrestling.

Dancing is the art of getting your feet out of the way faster than your partner can step on them.

Those who perform the modern dances exercise everything except discretion.

A jitterbug is not an insect. It's a human being acting like one.

The dance called the "twist" created an interesting phenomenon. For the first time in history, clothes were worn out from the inside.

A dancing foot and a praying knee seldom grow on the same body.

He who dances must pay the fiddler—also the waiter, the florist, the hatcheck girl, the doorman, and the parking attendant.

With some of these wild new dance steps, you don't know if the guy on the floor is a good dancer or a bad drunk.

DEATH

Some people have been dead for several years, but they just prefer not to have it known.

Death is not a period but a comma in the story of life.

No one is dead so long as he is remembered by someone.

When we die, we leave behind us all that we have and take with us all that we are.

People who are afraid of death are usually afraid of life.

Death is a black camel which kneels at the gates of all.

So live that when death comes, the mourners will outnumber the cheering section.

One easy way to die in the old days was to blow out the gas. The present way is to step on it.

As a rule, men do not die of disease but of internal combustion.

There are worse things than death—take life, for instance.

Make this your motto: Don't die until you are dead.

Natural death is now defined as being killed by an automobile.

A man, as he so lives, may die old at forty or young at eighty.

Everyone should fear death until he has something that will live on after his death.

DECISION

No one can grow by letting others make his decisions.

It's pretty hard for the Lord to guide a man if he hasn't made up his mind which way he wants to go.

If you're going to pull decisions out of a hat, be sure you are wearing the right hat.

Almost everybody knows the difference between right and wrong, but some hate to make decisions.

A man cannot go anywhere while he's straddling a fence.

Nothing great was ever done without an act of decision.

Always take plenty of time to make a snap decision.

Current events are so grim that we can't decide whether to watch the 6:00 news and not be able to eat, or the 10:00 news and not be able to sleep.

DEEDS

The smallest good deed is better than the grandest intention.

Superior to a kind thought is a kind word; better than both is a kind deed.

Good deeds speak for themselves. The tongue only interprets their eloquence.

He who does a kind deed should be silent; he who has received one should shout it from the housetop.

Small deeds done are better than great deeds planned.

Few people ever get dizzy from doing too many good turns.

There are a lot of people who never forget a kind deed—if they did it.

A good deed gets about as much attention these days as a homely face.

Some men are known by their deeds, others by their mortgages.

A kind deed often does more than a large gift.

DEFEAT

Defeat never comes to any man until he admits it.

Sometimes the most important fights are the ones you lose.

Defeat isn't bitter if you do not swallow it.

You are never defeated unless you defeat yourself.

He took his defeat like a man; he blamed it on his wife.

DIFFICULTIES

There are two ways of meeting difficulties: You alter the difficulties, or you alter yourself to meet them.

One of the most difficult mountains for people to climb is the one they make out of a molehill.

Tackle any difficulty at first sight, for the longer you gaze at it the bigger it grows.

The difficulties of life are intended to make us better—not bitter.

The most difficult thing to open is a closed mind.

DIGNITY

Dignity is one thing that cannot be preserved in alcohol.

The fellow who stands on his dignity finds he has poor footing.

It has been said that dignity is the stability to hold back on the tongue that which never should have been on the mind in the first place.

Many a man labors under the delusion that standing on his dignity will enable him to see over the heads of the crowd.

It is of very little use in trying to be dignified, if dignity is no part of your character.

Don't lean too heavily upon your dignity. It might let you down.

Many a man gets a reputation for dignity when he is merely suffering from a stiff neck.

DISAPPOINTMENTS

When we get what we want, we are always disappointed to find out it was not what we wanted.

Just about the time we think we can make both ends meet, somebody moves the ends.

Some of the most disappointed people in the world are those who get what is coming to them.

Disappointments should be cremated, not embalmed.

One of life's big disappointments is discovering that the man who writes the advertising for a bank is not the same guy who makes the loans.

Some of our biggest disappointments come from getting something we thought we wanted.

DISCRETION

Discretion is that something that comes to a person after he's too old for it to do him any good.

The age of discretion is when you make a fool of yourself in a more dignified way.

Discretion is putting two and two together and keeping your mouth shut.

Definition of discretion: Closing your eyes to a situation before someone else closes them for you.

DISSIPATION

America has many fine old ruins. Many of them may be found in our taverns and night clubs.

The higher you get in the evening, the lower you feel in the morning.

Cars and bars mean stars and scars.

Some people go around in circles, others get circles from going around.

Whether the cost of living goes up or down, the cost of "sowing wild oats" remains the same.

If you burn the candle at both ends you are not as bright as you may think.

The fellow who throws himself away probably won't like the place he lands.

Lots of people don't have to look at the world through rose-colored glasses. Their eyes are already bloodshot.

"Wild oats" take something out of the soil of one's life that no system of crop rotation can restore.

DIVORCE

Another thing this country needs is fewer self-made widows.

Divorce records show that many married couples spend too much time in court and not enough time courting.

A divorce is the refuge of those who do not favor a fight to the finish.

If people didn't get married for such silly reasons they wouldn't get divorced for such silly reasons.

A little common sense would prevent most divorces—and marriages, too.

Divorce is a custom so fashionable nowadays that really smart people are staying single in order to be different.

Many divorces are caused by the marriage to two people who are in love with themselves.

Divorce is the hash made from domestic scraps.

The divorce problem exists because there are too many married couples and too few husbands and wives.

One reason for the divorce evil is that people don't divorce evil.

Judging by the number of divorces, too many couples were mispronounced man and wife.

Love the quest, marriage the conquest, divorce the inquest.

There would be fewer divorces if the husband tried as hard to keep his wife as he did to get her.

Most divorces begin either because the wife talks too much or because the husband doesn't listen enough.

A man and his wife in Florida were divorced because of illness—they got sick of each other.

The way divorces keep climbing, some day the marriage ceremony will change from "I do" to "perhaps."

With as many divorces as we have nowadays, it seems that more parents are running away from home than children.

Judging by the divorce rate, a lot of people who said, "I do"—don't.

There would be fewer divorces if men gave as much loving attention to their wives as they do to their cars and boats.

The divorce rate would be lower if, instead of marrying for better or worse, people would marry for good.

There would be fewer divorces if women hunted husbands with as much thought as they hunt bargains.

DOUBT

If you doubt the propriety of doing a thing, you'd better give yourself the benefit of the doubt and not do it.

Many people believe their doubts and doubt their beliefs.

Doubt makes the mountain which faith can move.

When in doubt, tell the truth.

Feed your faith, and doubt will starve to death.

Some folks demand the benefit of the doubt when there isn't any.

When in doubt, don't.

DRUNKARDS

A drunkard is like a whisky bottle: All neck and belly and no head.

It is said that a drunkard drinks when he is thirsty to cure his thirst, and drinks when he is not thirsty to prevent it.

A drunkard can't make both ends meet because he is too busy making one end drink.

It is better that the drunkard be in the gutter than behind a steering wheel.

Pity the poor drunk who started out to get mellow, then he got ripe, and ended up rotten.

It's hard to tell some drunkards apart, they stagger so much.

A man is drunk when he feels sophisticated and can't pronounce it.

The man who drinks constantly is trying to pull himself out of trouble with a corkscrew.

A drinking man is the last man hired and the first man fired.

A weak moment with the bottle can mean several weeks in the jug.

The trouble with people who "drink like a fish" is they don't drink what the fishes drink.

DUTY

A lot of men always recognize their duty in sufficient time to sidestep it.

The best way to get rid of your duties is to discharge them.

When duty calls, some people are never at home.

Duty is a task we look forward to with distaste, perform with reluctance, and brag about afterwards.

A man never gets so confused in his thinking that he can't see the other fellow's duty.

Some people who do their duty as they see it need to consult an eye specialist.

You can do anything you ought to do.

Generally speaking, duty is what we expect of others.

God never imposes a duty without giving time and strength to perform it.

Many people spend more time trying to dodge duty than would be required to discharge it.

The fellow who believes he is exerting himself beyond the call of duty is apt to be a poor judge of distance.

A lot of people who see their duty look the other way.

E

EDUCATION

Among the few things costing more than an education today is the lack of it.

An educated man will sit up all night and worry over things a fool never dreamed of.

The sad part about education is that some of the final examinations are final.

You can buy education, but wisdom is a gift from God.

The true object of education should be to train one to think clearly and act rightly.

An educated man is one who knows a great deal and says little about it.

The money that is saved this year on education will be spent later on jails and reformatories.

Education can't make us all leaders, but it can teach us which leader to follow.

Speaking of higher education, here's hoping it doesn't go much higher.

It's what we learn after we know it all that really counts.

Education will broaden a narrow mind, but there is no known cure for a big head.

Those who don't read have no advantage over those who can't.

It is a pity so many people get college training without getting an education.

An educated man is one who has finally discovered that there are some questions to which nobody has the answer.

It is not what is poured into a student but what is planted that counts.

Education should include knowledge of what to do with it.

If a man's education is finished—he is finished.

Education is not a headfull of facts but knowing HOW and WHERE to find the facts.

Short-change your education now and you may be short of change the rest of your life.

May education never become as expensive as ignorance.

An education is one of the very few things a person is willing to pay for and not get.

Education is not "received." It is achieved.

When a boy goes to college, it's usually his father who gets an education.

Education pays unless you are an educator.

EGOTISM

Egotism is the glue with which you get stuck on yourself.

The emptiest man in all the world is the man who is full of himself.

One of the hardest secrets for a man to keep is his opinion of himself.

Egotism is the anesthetic that dulls the pain of stupidity.

Don't brag; it isn't the whistle that pulls the train.

Egotism is partly enthusiasm—but mostly ignorance.

As the chest swells, the brain and the heart shrinks.

When a man is wrapped up in himself, he makes a mighty small package.

A stiff neck usually supports an empty head.

The bouquet you hand yourself usually looks like weeds to the other fellow.

When a man tries himself, the verdict is usually in his favor.

Many a little squirt thinks he's a fountain of wisdom.

He who falls in love with himself will have no rivals.

Some people are like the rooster who thought the sun rises every morning just to hear him crow.

Egotism is a disease that often kills men before they know they have it.

The more you speak of yourself, the more you are likely to lie.

Some folks get carried away by the sound of their own voice—but not far enough.

One way to deflate your ego is to read the want ads and discover all the jobs you're not equipped to handle.

Some proud folks are always letting off esteem.

Those who are sold on themselves still have to find a buyer's market.

ENEMIES

Always speak well of your enemies, remember you made them.

If you want an enemy, just convince a fool that he is wrong.

When you bury the hatchet, don't bury it in your enemy's back.

The man you make for your enemy today may be the only one who can help you twenty-five years from now.

Nobody can have too many friends, but one enemy may constitute a surplus.

Love your enemies—it will drive them nuts.

It is possible to learn from an enemy things we cannot learn from our friends.

If you want enemies, excel your friends.

No enemy is more dangerous than a friend who isn't quite sure he is for you or against you.

If you simply must make enemies—pick lazy ones.

Some men make enemies instead of friends because it is less trouble.

The nice thing about your enemies is they don't try to borrow money from you.

Blessed are our enemies, for they tell us the truth when our friends flatter us.

Love your enemies, but if you really want to make them mad, ignore them completely.

ENTHUSIASM

He who has no fire in himself cannot warm others.

If it were as easy to arouse enthusiasm as it is suspicion, just think what could be accomplished!

Enthusiasm is a good engine, but it needs intelligence for a driver.

A wise man once said that enthusiasm is nothing but faith with a tin can tied to its tail.

Enthusiasm is infectious—and so is the lack of it.

We will not go very far without enthusiasm, but neither will we go very far if that is all we have.

Enthusiasm, most often, is apt to breed more action than accuracy.

There's always a good crop of food for thought. What we need is enough enthusiasm to harvest it.

Enthusiasm is that temper of the mind in which the imagination has gotten the better of judgment.

We have never learned to support the things we support with anything like the enthusiasm with which we oppose the things we oppose.

ENVY

Envy provides the mud that failure throws at success.

Don't envy anybody. Every person has something no other human being has. Develop that one thing and make it outstanding.

We under-rate that which we do not possess.

After a man makes his mark in the world, a lot of people will come around with erasers.

Envy is blind and knows nothing except to depreciate the excellence of others.

The only man worth envying is the one who has found a cause bigger than himself.

Every time you turn green with envy you are ripe for trouble.

Don't mind the fellow who belittles you; he's only trying to cut you down to his size.

ERROR

To err may be human, but to admit it isn't.

An error doesn't become a mistake until you refuse to correct it.

The longer a man is wrong, the surer he is he's right.

To err is human; to remain in error is stupid.

Things could be worse. Suppose your errors were counted and published every day like those of a baseball player?

It's true that to err is human—but it can be overdone.

EVIL

Supervising evil does not make it good.

All that is necessary for the triumph of evil is that good men do nothing.

A necessary evil is one we like so well we do not care about abolishing it.

Evil can never be disguised.

Man, being unable to choose between two evils, often hunts up a third.

Of two evils, when we are telling ourselves we are choosing the lesser, we usually mean we are choosing the more comfortable.

Evil flourishes in the world because the good people let their differences divide them instead of letting the things on which they agree unite them.

Evil often triumphs but it can never conquer.

Between two evils, choose neither; between two goods, choose both.

EXAMPLE

Always remember that there are certain people who set their watches by your clock.

None of us is entirely useless. Even the worst of us can serve as horrible examples.

The self-made man is usually a pathetic example of unskilled labor.

People seldom improve when they have no model but themselves.

The worst danger that confronts the younger generation is the example set by the older generation.

Every father should remember that one day his son will follow his example instead of his advice.

A good example is the best sermon.

We are less convinced by what we hear than by what we see.

What the world wants is not advice, but examples. Most any fool can talk.

How many people have made you homesick to know God?

People take your example far more seriously than they take your advice.

A great many children face the hard problem of learning good table manners without seeing any.

What can't be done by advice can often be done by example.

Example is a language all men can read.

It's often easier to set an example than a hen.

Foreign missionaries will be more successful when they can SHOW Christianity to the heathen and not merely tell them about it.

EXCUSES

When you don't want to do anything, one excuse is as good as another.

If you need some kind of an excuse, see your preacher; he has heard more than anybody else.

An excuse is a statement given to cover up for a duty not well done, or not done at all.

Never give an excuse that you would not be willing to accept.

If people would quit digging pits on Saturday night, there would not be so many oxen in the ditch on Sunday morning.

There aren't really enough crutches in the world for all the lame excuses.

The man who really wants to do something finds a way, the other kind finds an excuse.

There are always excuses available if you are weak enough to use them.

It is soon going to be too hot to do that job it was too cold to do last winter.

An excuse is usually a thin skin of falsehood stretched tightly over a bald-faced lie.

You can catch some men without money, sometimes without tobacco, but never without an excuse.

EXPERIENCE

Experience is one thing you can't get on the easy payment plan.

There is no way to get experience except through experience.

Experience increases our wisdom but doesn't seem to reduce our follies.

Some people speak from experience; others, from experience, don't speak.

It was bitter experience that put the "prod" into the prodigal son.

We all succeed. Some succeed at success; others succeed at failure.

One reason experience is such a good teacher is that she doesn't allow any dropouts.

If a man could sell his experiences for what they cost him, he would never need Social Security.

Don't expect to buy experience at a discount house.

Experience is a good school, but often the fees are high.

Every time you think you have graduated from the school of experience, somebody thinks up a new course.

Experience is what prevents you from making the same mistake again in exactly the same way.

The school of experience never changes; it always has and always will issue its diplomas on the roughest grade of sandpaper.

It requires experience to know how to use it.

One thorn of experience is worth a whole wilderness of warning.

Experience is a form of knowledge acquired in only two ways—by doing and by being done.

Some people have had nothing but experience.

A wise man learns by the experience of others. An ordinary man learns by his own experience. A fool learns by nobody's experience.

The class yell of the school of experience is "Ouch!"

F

FACTS

Facts do not cease to exist just because they are ignored.

It's easier to get facts than it is to face them.

Facts are troublesome things to the evil-doer.

Every man has a right to his opinion, but no man has a right to be wrong in his facts.

Facts mean nothing unless they are rightly understood, rightly related, and rightly interpreted.

People should keep their mouths shut and their pens dry until they can know the facts.

The next best thing to knowing a fact is knowing where to find it.

Facts apart from their relationships are like labels on an empty bottle.

When people agree as to what the facts are, they often disagree as to what the facts mean.

An ounce of fact means more than a ton of argument.

Fact is fact and feeling is feeling; never does the second change the first.

A thousand probabilities do not make one fact.

Digging for facts is much better than jumping to conclusions.

There's one thing for which you should be thankful—only you and God have all the facts about yourself.

Getting the facts is only half the job; the other half is to use them intelligently.

FAILURE

Stopping at third base adds no more to the score than striking out.

A failure in life is one who lives and fails to learn.

The only thing you can get for nothing is failure.

Life's greatest failure is failing to be true to the best you know.

A failure is a man who goes through life earning nothing but money.

The road to failure is greased with the slime of indifference.

Many people are not failures. They just started at the bottom and liked it there.

No man ever fails until he fails on the inside.

Failure is one thing that can be achieved without effort.

Better try something and fail, than try nothing and succeed.

Falling down doesn't make you a failure, but staying down does.

Formula for failure: Try to please everybody.

Failure is not necessarily missing the target, but aiming too low.

There are two kinds of failures: The man who will do nothing he is told, and the man who will do nothing else.

A failure is a man who has blundered and is not able to cash in on the experience.

FAITH

Faith is to the soul what a mainspring is to a watch.

You can do very little with faith, but you can do nothing without it.

In all relationships of life, faith is worthless unless it leads to action.

Faith makes the uplook good, the outlook bright, and the future glorious.

If your faith cannot move mountains, it ought to at least climb them.

We believe easily what we hope for earnestly.

The man who believes in nothing but himself lives in a very small world.

Some people have just enough faith to make them miserable, but not enough to make them happy and hopeful.

What is faith unless it is to believe what you do not see.

In believing in yourself, it is easy to overdo it.

Genuine faith is assuring, insuring, and enduring.

Faith believes all that God says even though circumstances seem to be against its fulfillment.

A person's faith is not judged by what he says about it, but by what he does about it.

When a man wants to believe something, it doesn't take much to convince him.

There is no better demonstration of faith than a man planting seeds in a field.

Faith is the daring of the soul to go farther than it can see.

It is a sickly faith that is shaken because some frail human being goes wrong.

Faith keeps the man who keeps his faith.

There are some whose faith is not strong enough to bring them to church services, but they expect it to take them to heaven.

All men need a faith that will not shrink when washed in the waters of affliction and adversity.

FAMILY TREES

Some families can trace their ancestry back three hundred years but can't tell you where their children were last night.

It takes about five years for a tree to produce nuts; but this doesn't apply to a family tree.

A good family tree is a useful object to climb into society with.

If we climb high enough up most any family tree we are likely to find something hanging there that is not an apple.

The best thing to do with the average family tree is to spray it.

Even the best family tree has its sap.

A family tree is something you pay a little to have looked up, and then pay more to have it hushed up.

One thing most family trees have in common is a shady branch.

What this country needs is more family trees that will produce more lumber and fewer nuts.

Most family trees have had at least one crop failure.

A grafter seldom improves the family tree.

FAULTFINDING

If faultfinding were electrified, some people would be a powerhouse.

Two things are bad for the heart—running up stairs and running down people.

Faultfinding is one talent that ought to be buried, and the place forgotten.

Don't find fault with what you don't understand.

Faultfinding is as dangerous as it is easy.

No rewards are offered for finding faults.

An expert faultfinder has no reason to be proud of his accomplishments.

FAULTS

Men and women have only two faults: What they say and what they do.

Some of us who have few faults make the most of what we've got.

Faults are thick where love is thin.

When looking for faults, use a mirror, not a telescope.

There are a lot of people in this world who would admit their faults—if they had any.

The greatest fault is to be conscious of none.

The easiest thing to find is fault.

Nature couldn't make us perfect, so she did the next best thing; she made us blind to our faults.

Most of us can live peacefully with our own faults, but the faults of others get on our nerves.

If you feel you have no faults—that makes another one.

A fault which humbles a man is of more use to him than a virtue which puffs him up.

If you must publish someone's faults, publish your own.

Few people have good enough sight to see their own faults.

The faults of others are like headlights on a passing car. They all seem more glaring than your own.

Rare is the person who can weigh the faults of others without putting his thumb on the scales.

FLATTERY

Flattery is hearing from others the things you have already thought about yourself.

Many people soft-soap their friends until they can't see for the suds.

A little flattery now and then often makes husbands out of single men.

Flattery will get you nowhere. This is especially true when you give it to yourself.

However much one may scoff at flattery, deep down in his heart he is pleased with the thought that some of it might be true.

Flattery makes you think you are better than you are, and no living person can be that.

If flattery is the food of fools, why are we so starved for it?

Flattery is like perfume; you are supposed to smell it, not swallow it.

FOOLS

Some people can't wait until April to make fools of themselves.

Fools rush in where angels wouldn't even send a calling card.

No law has ever been passed that will keep a man from acting a fool.

We know that a fool and his money are soon parted, but how did they ever get together?

Preachers and lawyers are paid for zeal; but fools dish it out for nothing.

If anybody calls you a fool, don't insist on his proving it. He might do it.

No woman ever made a fool out of a man without at least some cooperation.

There are so many different ways of being a fool that no man can hope to dodge all of them.

There is no fool like an old fool. You just can't beat experience.

Twin fools: One doubts nothing, the other doubts everything.

Nobody can make a fool out of another person if he isn't the right kind of material for the job.

A fool and a drunkard are two of the most mistaken human beings on earth. One thinks he is wise, and the other thinks he is sober.

Many people display a lot of unexpected talent when it comes to acting a fool.

It's bad to act like a fool but it's worse when you're not acting.

Women make fools of some men. Other men are the do-it-yourself type.

A fool is simply a person whose brand of folly differs from your own.

FORGIVENESS

After a good dinner, one can forgive anybody, even one's relatives.

It is far better to forgive and forget than to hate and remember.

Always forgive your enemies; nothing annoys them quite so much.

Forgiveness saves the expense of anger and the cost of hatred.

We should forgive and then forget what we have forgiven.

It's much easier to forgive an enemy after you have gotten even with him.

Forgiveness is the perfume that the trampled flower casts back upon the heel that crushed it.

We are most like beasts when we kill. We are most like men when we judge. We are most like God when we forgive.

FRIENDS

Credit and friends are good when not used.

Friends are those who speak to you after others don't.

A friend is like a dollar—hard to get and easy to throw away.

Before you need them is the time to make friends.

It's smart to pick your friends—but not to pieces.

Friends are like radios—some have volume and some have tone.

A man never gets so rich that he can afford to lose a friend.

A friend whom you can buy can be bought from you.

False friends are those who roll out the carpet for you one day—and pull it out from under you the next day.

A friend takes an interest in you—but not a controlling one.

Constant use will wear away anything—especially friends.

It seems that a friend in need is about the only kind a person has these days.

You never know how many friends you have until you rent a cottage on the beach.

The friends you make in prosperity are those you lose in adversity.

Our best investment is not in funds but friends.

Sometimes a close friend really is when you ask him for a loan.

A friend is one who walks in when the rest of the world walks out.

It's better to make friends fast than to make fast friends.

In order for two people to be friends one will have to be patient.

You can't cultivate a friend by digging up dirt around him.

A friend is one who is thinking of you, when all others are thinking of themselves.

Having money and friends is easy. Having friends and no money is an accomplishment.

Promises may get friends, but it is performance that keeps them.

It is so true that a real friend never gets in your way—unless you happen to be on the way down.

Knock your friends often enough, and soon you'll find no one at home.

FRIENDSHIP

Broken friendships may be patched up, but the patch is likely to show.

Another good way to preserve friendship—don't work it to death.

The bank of friendship cannot exist for long without deposits.

You can only extend the hand of friendship; you cannot force the other fellow to grasp it.

Genuine friendship is like sound health, the value of it is seldom known until it is lost.

The quickest way to wipe out a friendship is to sponge on it.

Friendship that is bought will not stay bought, for sooner or later there will be a higher bidder.

Friendships cemented together with sin do not hold.

The best way to be sure of a man's friendship is not to put it to the test.

Friendships last when each friend thinks he has a slight superiority over the other.

A friendship that makes the least noise is often the most useful.

Friendship is a living thing that lasts only as long as it is nourished with kindness, sympathy, and understanding.

FUTURE

It's a good idea to take an interest in the future—that's where you will spend the rest of your life.

Hats off to the past, coats off to the future.

Perhaps the best thing about the future is that it only comes one day at a time.

We make our future by the best use of the present.

Those who remember the past with a clear conscience need have no fear of the future.

Don't take tomorrow to bed with you.

Never be afraid to trust an unknown future to a known God.

If you've mortgaged the future to buy folly, don't complain when the foreclosure comes.

Whatever your past has been, you have a spotless future.

Those who fear the future are likely to fumble the present.

The trouble with the future is that it usually arrives before we're ready for it.

Future generations will be born free, equal and in debt.

Some folks are so far behind, the future is gone before they get there.

The future holds something in store for the individual who keeps faith in it.

More people worry about the future than those who prepare for it.

G

GAMBLING

The best throw of the dice is to throw them away.

When walking across the street, motoring, or flying, don't gamble—you can't afford to lose.

No horse can go as fast as the money you bet on him.

The first time a man bets he bets to win. The rest of the time he's trying to get even.

He who hopes to win what belongs to another deserves to lose his own.

A person who will gamble with money will gamble with his soul.

The most dangerous wheel of chance is the steering wheel.

Playing with dice is a shaky business.

The safest bet is the one you didn't make.

Gambling is just plain stealing by mutual consent.

You do not really make money in the stock market. You merely take it from somebody who guessed wrong.

People who can afford to gamble don't need money, and those who need money can't afford to gamble.

Gambling is frequently a means of getting nothing for your money.

GENTLEMEN

One of the marks of a gentleman is his refusal to make an issue out of every difference of opinion.

A gentleman is a man who is always as nice as he sometimes is.

The real gentleman is the fellow who is courteous and affable even when not trying to sell you something.

To be a gentleman is a worthy trait, but it is a great handicap in an argument.

There is only one way to be a gentleman—there are hundreds of ways not to be.

If a man cannot be a gentleman where he is he cannot be a gentleman anywhere.

The final test of a gentleman is his respect for those who can be of no possible service to him.

A gentlemen is a man who has had the same operation but says nothing.

The first duty of a gentleman is to put back into the world at least the equivalent of what he has taken out of it.

GIVING

Don't give till it hurts—give till it feels good.

Support the church with your money. You can't take it with you but you can send it on ahead.

Blessed are those who can give without remembering, and receive without forgetting.

Many people give a tenth to the Lord—a tenth of what they should give.

Give with no strings attached, and you will receive in the same manner.

A great many church members put zero into the collection plate and then complain that the service was cold.

Giving is grace, not giving is disgrace.

The Lord loves a cheerful giver—until he brags about it.

Where there is no interest, there is no investment.

There are many nerves in the human body, but the most sensitive is the one that goes from the brain to the pocketbook.

The way some people give, you would think the church is coin-operated.

When a man's heart is in heaven, it does not suffer from palpitation every time he sees the collection plate coming.

He who gives only when he is asked has waited too long.

The world is composed of the takers and the givers. The takers may eat better, but the givers sleep better.

Feel for others—in your pocketbook.

The hardest thing to give is IN.

When it comes to giving until it hurts, most of us have a very low threshold of pain.

Give not from the top of your purse, but from the bottom of your heart.

A collection at a church service is that in which many take but a passing interest.

Too many friends of the church are CLOSE friends.

From the amount that some people give to the Lord, they are positive that it is the little things that count.

It may be more blessed to give than to receive but it sure costs more.

Some give their mite; some give with all their might; and some don't give who might.

GOD

When we do what we can, God will do what we can't.

Many people want God's blessings, but they don't want Him.

God shocked the world with a Babe, not a bomb.

It should be a great comfort to know that God still has His hands on the steering wheel of the universe.

When God measures a man, he puts the tape around the heart instead of the head.

God still speaks to those who take the time to listen.

If God is kept outside, something must be wrong inside.

Many people want an affidavit from God that He really exists.

When you get to the end of your rope, be thankful—God is there.

God has been around a long time and intends to stay.

Whatever God wants us to do, He will help us do it.

Our Lord cannot go forth to war with an army of tin soldiers.

Sooner or later we must learn that God makes no deals.

The promises of God are certain, but they do not all mature in ninety days.

To fear God is to reverence Him, respect Him, and acknowledge Him.

God often visits us, but most of the time we are not at home.

You are not obligated to put on evening clothes to meet God.

It is utterly impossible for any person to demonstrate that there is no God.

Our Lord is in the cleansing business, not the whitewashing business.

God never gives you anything bigger to do than you have resources to handle.

The birth of every baby is God's vote of confidence in the future of man.

God is never more than a prayer away from you.

If God is small enough for us to understand, He isn't big enough for us to worship.

God never intended that we do as we please, but as He pleases.

GOLDEN RULE

The Golden Rule is what we want everybody else to practice.

One of the troubles in the world today is that we have allowed the Golden Rule to tarnish.

We commit the Golden Rule to memory and forget to commit it to life.

Do unto others as though you were the others.

You seldom hear of a mob rushing across town to support the Golden Rule.

The Golden Rule may be old but it hasn't been used enough to show much signs of wear.

Practicing the Golden Rule is not a sacrifice; it is an investment.

The trouble with the Golden Rule is that before men are ready to live by it they have lead in their legs and silver in their hair.

GOODNESS

The only way to be good is to obey God, love your fellow men and hate the devil.

There isn't a man alive who is as good as he knows he ought to be.

Be not simply good—be good for something.

Goodness consists not so much in the outward things we do, but in the inward things we are.

We do more good by being good than in any other way.

There is some good in everyone, though in some it takes a little longer to find it.

Some people are never good except when they are feeling bad.

There is no limit to the amount of good a man can do if he doesn't care who gets the credit.

There must be a lot of good in some folks, because none of it ever comes out.

GOSSIP

Gossip is sometimes referred to as halitosis of the mind.

Much gossip that is aired should also be fumigated.

Gossip is one form of crime for which the law provides no punishment.

Some folks think the statement, "it is more blessed to give than to receive," has reference only to gossip.

If we all said to people's faces what we say behind each other's backs, society would be impossible.

Gossip is like mud thrown on a clean wall. It may not stick but it always leaves a dirty mark.

You can't believe everything you hear—but you can repeat it.

Common gossip is a symptom of an empty mind and a carrion-loving heart.

It is always hard to sling mud with clean hands.

The expert gossiper knows just how much to leave out of a conversation.

Gossip is when someone gets wind of something and treats it like a cyclone.

If it goes in one ear and out the mouth—it's gossip.

Gossip is the fine art of saying nothing in such a way that leaves practically nothing unsaid.

Without tale-hearers there would be no tale-bearers.

There's a fortune awaiting any man who can find something to do with gossip besides repeating it.

Gossip is like a balloon—it grows bigger with every puff.

Talking about others and being a gossip is probably better than talking about yourself and being a bore.

GRATITUDE

He who is not grateful for the good things he has would not be happy with what he wishes he had.

If you can't be grateful for what you receive; be grateful for what you escape.

How many who wrote Santa Claus before Christmas wrote him a thank-you note after Christmas?

Be grateful for your doors of opportunity—and for friends who oil the hinges.

If you have nothing to be thankful for, make up your mind that there is something wrong with you.

GROUCHES

A grouch thinks the world is against him—and it is.

The trouble with being a grouch is that you have to make a new set of friends every few months.

A grouch never goes where he is told until he dies.

We all know that sourness spoils milk—and it has the same effect on human beings.

Sometimes a reprimand is only a grouch in disguise.

A grouch is a guy who has sized himself up and got sore about it.

Did you hear about the grouch who had three telephones so he could hang up on more people?

GRUDGES

A grudge is too heavy a load for any man to carry.

No matter how long you nurse a grudge it won't get better.

Nursing a grudge is like arguing with a cop. The more you do it the worse things get.

GRUMBLING

It requires no musical talent always to be harping on something.

Some grumble because they don't get what's coming to them, others because they do.

When you get the daily bread you have been praying for, do not grumble because it is not cake.

A grumbler always complains about the noise when opportunity knocks.

H

HABITS

Habits are like a soft bed, easy to get into but hard to get out of.

We should get the habit of putting things over—not off.

The best way to break a habit is to drop it.

A bad habit is first a caller, then a guest, and then a master.

Chains of habit are usually too small to be felt until they become too strong to be broken.

Good habits are usually formed. Bad habits we fall into.

If there's anything harder than breaking a bad habit, it's trying to tell how you did it.

It's easier to form good habits than reform bad ones.

Habits are either the best of servants or the worst of masters.

Changing our habits, like climbing a long flight of stairs, is something we do easier when we are young.

HAPPINESS

A lot of happiness is overlooked because it doesn't cost anything.

Basis for happiness: Something to do; something to love; something to look forward to.

People are generally about as happy as they have made up their minds to be.

Do something every day to make other people happy, even if it's only to let them alone.

The surest steps toward happiness are the church steps. Tread them often.

Happiness is like a potato salad—when shared with others, it's a picnic.

If happiness could be bought, most of us would be unhappy because of the price.

Happiness is getting something you want but didn't expect.

No one can define happiness. You have to be unhappy to understand it.

The secret of happiness is to count your blessings while others are adding up their troubles.

It's a pity that happiness isn't as easy to find as trouble.

The place to be happy is here, the time to be happy is now, the way to be happy is to make others so.

You will be happier if you will give people a bit of your heart rather than a piece of your mind.

Real happiness is cheap enough, yet how dearly we pay for its counterfeit.

The heart is happiest that beats for others.

You can't sprinkle the perfume of happiness on others without getting a few drops on yourself.

Happiness does not come from what you have, but from what you are.

High-octane happiness is a blend of gratitude, service, friendship and contentment.

Some people find happiness by making the most of what they don't have.

Pursuing happiness would be a lot easier if everybody slowed down a little.

HATRED

Hate hurts the hater more than the hated.

Two people can't hate each other if both love God.

Hatred is like a rifle with a plugged barrel. The backfire can be much more dangerous than the shot.

If you want to be miserable, hate somebody.

Hate is a luxury no one can afford.

Hatred does a great deal more damage to the vessel in which it is stored than the object on which it is poured.

Doctors tell us that hating people can cause ulcers, heart attacks, headaches, skin rashes and asthma. It doesn't make the people we hate feel too good either.

Hatred is cancer of the intellect.

We should never permit ourselves to stoop so low as to hate any human being.

Hate or a deep-seated hostility is the most inefficient use a person can make of his mind.

HEAVEN

The distance from earth to heaven is not so much a matter of altitude as it is attitude.

Going to heaven is like riding a bicycle—you must either go on or get off.

The man who expects to go to heaven must take the time to study the route that will get him there.

You can't get into heaven by naturalization papers.

The way to heaven is to turn right and keep straight.

Some people want to go to heaven for the same reason they want to go to California—they have relatives there.

The average person probably hasn't stored up enough treasure in heaven to make the down payment on a harp.

He who seldom thinks of heaven is not likely to get there.

The road to heaven is never over-crowded.

Many a person's idea of heaven would be nothing to do and an eternity to do it in.

Some people talk about heaven being so far away. It is within speaking distance to those who belong there.

Almost everybody is in favor of going to heaven, but too many people are hoping they'll live long enough to see an easing of the entrance requirements.

If you wish to dwell in the house of many mansions, you must make your reservation in advance.

The ladder to heaven is let down just where you are. Begin to climb at once.

Many people hope to be elected to heaven who are not even running for the office.

Heaven is a place many Americans wouldn't want to go if they couldn't send back picture post cards.

When you get to heaven you will be surprised to see many people there you did not expect to see. Many may be surprised to see you there, too!

There is no reaching heaven except by traveling the only path that leads there.

HOME

Money can build a house, but it takes love to make it a home.

A home is not always what you make it; neighbors make it noisy, friends mess it up, and the landlord makes it expensive.

Homes are like banks—they go broke if you take out more than you put in.

There is no place like home where we are treated the best and grumble the most.

It seems that many people these days are building new homes on the outskirts of their incomes.

A model house isn't worth much without a model family inside.

Some wit has said that the easiest way to feel at home is to stay there.

Two things make unhappy homes—men's love for wet goods and women's love for dry goods.

Every human being should have three homes: A domestic home, a church home, and an eternal home.

Our greatest need today is for more home-builders and fewer home-wreckers.

A happy home is one in which each spouse grants the possibility that the other may be right, though neither believes it.

It takes a heap 'o livin to make a house a home, but before that, it takes a heap of borrowin'.

Home is a place where a man is free to say and do anything he pleases, because no one will pay the slightest attention to him.

The most essential element in any home is God.

A real home is more than just a roof over your head—it's a foundation under your feet.

Many of the homes nowadays seem to be on three shifts—father is on the night shift, mother is on the day shift, and the children shift for themselves.

In most homes it's a fifty-fifty proposition. The husband tells the wife what to do, and the wife tells the husband where to go.

HONESTY

Honesty is not the best policy—it is the only policy.

It takes a mighty honest man to tell the difference between when he's tired and when he's just plain lazy.

No one will ever know of your honesty unless you give out some samples.

Common honesty should be more common.

There are no degrees of honesty.

It is better to be honest in one language than a liar in five.

Honesty is one business policy that will never have to be changed to keep up with the times.

Nobody ever got hurt on the corners of a square deal.

All men are honest—until they are faced with a situation big enough to make them dishonest.

After all, honesty may be the best policy because it has so little competition.

It pays to be honest. It pays even more than it costs.

The world will be a better place in which to live when the "found" ads in the newspapers begin to outnumber the "lost" ads.

A policy of absolute honesty can be the making of a man's character and the ruination of his golf game.

When you sell yourself, be sure that you don't misrepresent the goods.

HOPE

Hope springs eternal in the human heart, but with some the spring is getting very weak.

There are those who cast their bread upon the waters hoping it will be returned toasted and buttered.

People no longer hope for the best. They just hope to avoid the worst.

Hope sees the invisible, feels the intangible, and achieves the impossible.

You can't live on hope, nor can you live without it.

Lost hope is the undertaker's best friend.

We may as well hope for the best, be prepared for the worst, and take what comes with a grin.

There's more hope for a self-confessed sinner than a self-conceited saint.

HUMILITY

Humility is that strange thing that the moment you think you have it, you have lost it.

The person with true humility never has to be shown his place; he is always in it.

It may be well to stand tall in this life, but heaven is entered only on the knees.

Those traveling the highway of humility won't be bothered by any heavy traffic.

Humility is the ability to act embarrassed while you tell people how wonderful you are.

The man who bows humbly before God is sure to walk upright before men.

Stay humble or stumble.

The best way to be right or wrong is humbly.

A wise man once said that humility is Christian clothing: It never goes out of style.

Humility and self-denial are always admired but seldom practiced.

He is without humility who sees it within himself.

Humility makes a man feel smaller as he becomes greater.

Too many people are humble—and know it.

Humility is one of the qualities left out of a self-made man.

HYPOCRITES

An actor is the only honest hypocrite.

It takes a man smaller than a hypocrite to hide behind one.

If a hypocrite is between you and God, he is closer to God than you are.

A hypocrite is like a pin—points one way and heads another.

The person who preaches by the yard but practices by the inch is a hypocrite.

A hypocrite at least appreciates goodness enough to imitate it.

If you cause a man to think he is right when he is wrong, you are a hypocrite.

A hypocrite prays on his knees on Sunday—and on his neighbors the rest of the week.

I

IDEALS

Most of us have high ideals and will stand by them as long as it pays.

A man's true ideals are those he lives by, not always those he talks about.

If you are satisfied with yourself you had better change your ideals.

The hope is that some day the Christian ideal will be put into practice.

Ideals may be beyond our reach but never beyond our fondest hopes.

Our ideals are too often like an antique chair—nice to talk about and show off but too fragile to use.

Keep your ideals high enough to inspire you, but low enough to encourage you.

If we cannot fulfill our own ideals we cannot expect others to accept them.

IDEAS

Ideas are funny things. They don't work unless you do.

There are more warmed over ideas than hot ones.

Good ideas need landing gear as well as wings.

The reason ideas die quickly in some heads is because they can't stand solitary confinement.

You are certain to get the worst of the bargain when you exchange ideas with a fool.

The real test of a good idea is whether or not it is your own.

Ideas are like rivets. They should be driven home and clenched while hot.

The normal reaction to a new idea is to think of reasons why it can't be done.

Some folks entertain ideas; others work them.

In many ways, ideas are more important than people—they are more permanent.

Ideas are very much like children—your own are wonderful.

How good a red hot idea is usually depends on how much heat it loses when somebody throws cold water on it.

It is better to have no ideas at all than to have false ones.

You can kill men and cripple nations, but you cannot kill an idea.

Many a good idea has been smothered to death by words.

Good ideas are subjected to solitary confinement when they get into an empty head.

A good idea poorly expressed often sounds like a poor one.

IDLENESS

The hardest job of all is trying to look busy when you are not.

Most of the people who sit around waiting for the harvest haven't planted anything.

Footprints on the sands of time were not made sitting down.

The man who has nothing to do always gives it his personal attention.

There are more idle brains than idle hands.

Doing nothing is the most tiresome job in the world because you can't quit and rest.

Stand still and watch the world go by—and it will.

When a man sits down to wait for his ship to come in, it usually turns out to be a receivership.

A loafer is always glad when Monday comes. He has another whole week to loaf.

Idleness is the nest in which mischief lays its eggs.

The chief reward for idleness is poverty.

Idleness travels so slowly that poverty soon overtakes it.

When an idler sees a completed job, he is sure he could have done it better.

Don't wait for your ship to come in if you haven't sent one out.

IGNORANCE

When Mother Nature distributed brains, a lot of her children must have been absent.

Ignorance needs no introduction; it always makes itself known.

Poverty is no disgrace, but ignorance is.

It's not necessary for some people to put out the light to be in the dark.

What you don't know won't hurt you, but it may make you look pretty silly.

The only thing more expensive than education is ignorance.

If ignorance is bliss, why aren't more people happy?

The darkest ignorance is man's ignorance of God.

There is nothing more terrifying than ignorance in action.

It seems that some people were born ignorant—and later had a relapse.

A person can accumulate a lot of ignorance in the course of a lifetime.

It is better to be silent and be thought dumb than to speak and remove all doubt.

IMPROVEMENT

Improvement is what you see a need of in other people, but can't see the same need in yourself.

People seldom improve when they have no model but themselves to copy after.

The world might be improved with less television and a lot more vision.

Nobody ever does his best; that is why we all have a good chance to do better.

One way to make the world better is by improving yourself.

Looking into the mirror isn't exactly the best way to convince yourself that certain things are improving.

INFLUENCE

Influence is something you THINK you have until you try to use it.

Just one act of yours may turn the tide of another person's life.

You can never bury your influence.

A man lives as long as there are those who bear the stamp of his influence.

One sure way for you to gain adherents for your cause is to start winning.

To judge the real importance of an individual, we should think of the effect his death would produce.

It is impossible for you to influence others to a higher level than that on which you live yourself.

INTELLIGENCE

Intelligence is like a river, the deeper it is the less noise it makes.

Brains and religion make a combination that's hard to beat.

Human intelligence is thousands of years old but it doesn't seem to act its age.

The only substitute for brains is silence.

A lot of people are smarter than they look—and they ought to be.

The difference between education and intelligence is that intelligence will make you a living.

Don't always assume that the other person has equal intelligence—he might have more.

It is incredible how much intelligence is used in this world to prove nonsense.

The bad thing about you looking at anything from a sensible angle is that it makes you so unpopular.

There is no limit to either intelligence or ignorance.

J

JUDGING

Never judge a man by his relatives; he did not choose them.

It is a mistake to try to judge a man's horsepower by the size of his exhaust.

The best way to judge a man is not by what other men say about him, but by what he says about other men.

It is easy to misconstrue the actions and words of those we dislike.

You will make a mistake if you judge a man by his opinion of himself.

Too many people are unable to judge as to what a man is on account of what he has.

It's easier to judge people by what they fall for than by what they stand for.

Never judge a man's actions until you know his motives.

You can judge a man not only by the company he keeps, but by the jokes he tells.

Don't judge a man by the clothes he wears; God made one, the tailor the other.

You can't depend on your evaluation of a person when your imagination is out of focus.

Don't judge a man by what he says, try and find out WHY he said it.

JUDGMENT

The judgment of no man is better than his information.

Don't condemn the judgment of another because it differs from your own. You both may be wrong.

Snap judgment would be all right if it didn't come unsnapped so often.

Rare is the man who regularly is governed by sound judgment.

The best some of us can expect on the Day of Judgment is a suspended sentence.

Don't trust your wife's judgment—look at whom she married!

JUSTICE

Justice is what we get when the decision is in our favor.

If a cause is just it will eventually triumph in spite of all the propaganda issued against it.

Justice is blind, but seldom is it too blind to distinguish between the defendant who has a roll and the one who is dead broke.

Everybody is for justice, thinking it will bring him rewards and bring his neighbors what they have coming to them.

There's justice for all, but it doesn't seem to be equally distributed.

Justice is something that is too good for some people and not good enough for others.

It is just as well that justice is blind; she might not like some of the things done in her name if she could see them.

JUVENILE DELINQUENCY

Every boy, in his heart, would rather steal second base than an automobile.

One way to curb juvenile delinquency is to take the parents off the streets at night.

Juvenile delinquency is a modern term for what we did when we were kids.

All that the overwhelming majority is doing about juvenile delinquency is reading about it.

There seems to be a juvenile problem of children running away from home. It is entirely possible they may be looking for their parents.

In the days when a woodshed stood behind the American home, a great deal of what passes as juvenile delinquency today was settled out of court.

Delinquent children are children who have reached the age when they want to do what papa and mama are doing.

No enemy nation could afford to take the risk of invading our country. Our juvenile delinquents are too well armed.

Another trouble with juvenile delinquency is that it's harder to say than cussedness.

When a youth begins to sow wild oats it's time for father to start the threshing machine.

Very few old people are qualified to discourse on juvenile delinquency. They have been away from it too long.

There would be less juvenile delinquency if parents led the way instead of pointing to it.

Do you remember the good old days when a juvenile delinquent was a boy who played the saxophone too loud?

The favorite cereal of juvenile delinquents is wild oats.

Most juvenile delinquents are youngsters who have been given a free hand, but not in the proper place.

In the old days kids cut classes instead of teachers.

Juvenile delinquency is like charity—it begins at home.

A juvenile delinquent usually prefers vice to advice.

One reason for juvenile delinquency is that parents are raising their children by remote control.

Happy laughter and family voices in the home will keep more kids off the streets at night than the loudest curfew.

K

KINDNESS

Kindness is the oil that takes the friction out of life.

The milk of human kindness never curdles.

This is a dangerous age but you don't stand in much danger of being killed by kindness.

No man is too big to be kind, but many men are too little.

Be as kind as you can today; tomorrow you may not be here.

Kindness is the golden chain by which society is bound together.

Most people will overlook the faults of anyone who is kind.

Remember, there has never been an over-production of kind words.

The man who sows seeds of kindness enjoys a perpetual harvest.

If a person is killed by kindness, the chances are it should come under the heading of accidental death.

Learn to say kind words—nobody resents them.

The kindness planned for tomorrow doesn't count today.

It's too bad that so many folks in passing out the milk of human kindness always skim it first.

Kindness pays most when you don't do it for pay.

A kindness done today is the surest way to brighten tomorrow.

Never part without loving words. They might be your last.

Better a little kindness while living, than an extravagant floral display at the grave.

Money will buy a fine dog, but only kindness will make him wag his tail.

Kindness is a language which the deaf can hear and the blind can read.

Remember the kindness of others; forget your own.

KNOCKING

The world would be a lot better if we would let opportunity do all the knocking.

Hard knocks won't hurt you—unless you're doing all the knocking.

If you're still knocking your church, why not check to see if it has improved any since the last time you were there?

A knocker is often a man who is in debt to the folks he is hammering on.

Now if they would only invent anti-knock gas for people!

If one chooses to be a knocker, he needs neither brains nor education.

Sometimes we don't know who is knocking—opportunity or temptation.

Knocking is a sign of either carbon or envy.

A knocker is like a cat fish—all mouth and no brains.

It isn't necessary to blow out the other person's light to let your own shine.

A chronic knocker never goes where he is told to go until he dies.

There should be more men laying bricks and fewer throwing them.

Have you noticed that most knocking is done by folks who don't know how to ring the bell?

KNOWLEDGE

No one is ever too old to learn, but many people keep putting it off.

It is not so much what we know as how we use what we know.

Knowledge humbles great men, astonishes the common man, and puffs up the little man.

A good listener is not only popular, but after awhile he knows something.

The only commodity on earth that does not deteriorate with use is knowledge.

Some people get the point too soon and therefore never learns anything.

You may know more than your employer, but his knowledge pays off.

The fact that you know what to say does not guarantee your right or obligation to say it.

You may not know all the answers, but you probably won't be asked all the questions, either.

The best part of our knowledge is that which teaches us where knowledge leaves off and ignorance begins.

Some students drink at the fountain of knowledge. Others just gargle.

The elevator operator has his ups and downs, but he is one of the few who knows where he is going.

Some people have a great curiosity to know everything except what is worth knowing.

Knowledge not reduced to practice is useless.

Those who really thirst for knowledge always get it.

If you want to know how to handle a big fortune, ask the man who has none.

The first step to knowledge is to know that you are ignorant.

What you don't know you can learn.

The only thing that doesn't become second-hand through use is knowledge.

Knowledge advances by steps, not by leaps.

Although psychologists say man is afraid of the unknown—it is some of the stuff we know that really scares us.

Knowledge is like a snapshot. It can be enlarged, but if it gets out of focus, everything will become a blur.

It is impossible for anyone to begin to learn what he thinks he already knows.

What you don't know doesn't hurt you—until you find out someone else is getting paid for knowing what you don't.

L

LAUGHTER

There is always something to laugh about every day, even if it is only about yourself.

If the world laughs at you, laugh right back—it's as funny as you.

Laugh with people—not at them.

Without fools and politicians the people would have but little to laugh at.

Don't laugh at the fallen; there may be slippery places in your path.

Laughter is to life what salt is to an egg.

Try if you can to make the world laugh; it already has enough to cry about.

What you laugh at tells plainer than words what you are.

When you laugh, be sure to laugh at what people do and not what they are.

Blessed is the man who can laugh at himself. He'll never cease to be amused.

LAZINESS

Some people do nothing in particular; but they do it very well.

Laziness is a good deal like money; the more a man has of it the more he seems to want.

Too many people itch for what they want, but won't scratch for it.

The only bright spots in some men's lives are on the seat of their pants.

Laziness is a quality that prevents people from getting tired.

People who sit around and wait for their ship to come in usually find that it is hardship.

While some are standing on the promises, others just sit on the premises.

The fellow who fiddles around seldom gets to lead the orchestra.

There's no cure for laziness in a man, but a wife and children help some.

Laziness is an overwhelming love for physical calm.

The lazier a man is, the more he is going to do tomorrow.

Everybody likes spring because they can then call plain laziness spring fever.

Entirely too many people fashion their lives after French bread—one long loaf!

The thing that worries the boss is the number of unemployed still on the pay roll.

LEADERSHIP

He who is a leader of men is rarely a follower of women.

The climax of leadership is to know WHEN to do WHAT.

If a man has never been over the road himself, do not accept him as a leader to show you the way.

A leader is anyone who has two characteristics: First, he is going somewhere; second, he is able to persuade other people to go with him.

You can't lead someone any farther than you have gone yourself.

The trouble with being a leader today is that you can't be sure people are following or chasing you.

We herd sheep; we drive cattle; we lead men.

The world would be happier if its leaders had more vision and fewer nightmares.

A good leader takes a little more than his share of the blame; a little less than his share of credit.

The business of a leader is to turn weakness into strength; obstacles into stepping stones, and disaster into triumph.

One of the best tests of leadership is the ability to recognize a problem before it becomes an emergency.

A true leader faces the music even when he dislikes the tune.

LIARS

If a man is a liar it is useless to tell him so. He knew it all the time.

There are some people so addicted to exaggeration they can't tell the truth without lying.

No man has a good enough memory to be a successful liar.

The most mischievous liars are those who keep sliding on the verge of truth.

A liar is usually not believed even when he speaks the truth.

No man is a successful liar unless someone believes him.

A liar is one hard not to believe when he says nice things about us.

Which has made the biggest liars out of Americans—golf or the income tax?

The only thing that keeps some people from being bald-faced liars is their moustache.

There are many people who are not actually liars, but they keep a respectful distance from the truth.

LIBERTY

Where food is free, liberty isn't.

It's not the liberty we have, but the liberty we take, which causes most of the trouble.

There is no liberty worth anything which is not liberty under law.

Let's not fight for more liberty until we learn to handle what we've got.

Personal liberty ends where public safety begins.

Every person has the liberty to do that which is good, just, and honest.

The pioneers who fought for their liberties now have descendants who take them.

Liberty is the right to go just as far as the law allows.

If ever a new Statue of Liberty is designed, it will be holding the bag instead of the torch.

What this country needs is not more liberty, but fewer people who take liberties with liberty.

LIES

The fellow who says he has never told a lie has just told one.

A lie may take care of the present, but it has no future.

It is easy to tell one lie but hard to tell only one.

The most dangerous lies are those that most resemble the truth.

With many people, telling lies is not only a shortcoming, but it is one of their major accomplishments.

The trouble with the little white lie is that it not only grows but changes color.

A lie has always a certain amount of weight with those who wish to believe it.

The devil is the father of lies, but he forgot to patent the idea.

A good memory is needed, once you have lied.

There are three things that cannot lie: The smile of a baby, the wag of a dog's tail, and figures.

Lies, like chickens, come home to roost.

Nothing lends the weight of truth to a lie like saying it in a whisper.

The man who always agrees with you lies to others also.

Many people don't actually lie; they merely present the truth in such a way that nobody recognizes it.

LIFE

When all the affairs of life are said and done, there is more said than done.

Life is tragic for him who has plenty to live on and nothing to live for.

If your life is an open book, don't bore your friends by reading out of it.

About the time we learn to make the most of life, the greater part of it is gone.

If your life is empty, why not put Christ into it?

Life is like a mirror—we get the best results when we smile at it.

It isn't how high you go in life that counts, but HOW you got there.

A long life is a gift of God; a full and fruitful life is your own doing.

Take life as you find it, but don't leave it so.

How tragic to give one's life to something the world does not need.

Life is somewhat like a camel. You can make it do anything except back up.

Some people don't go through life—they're merely shoved through it.

In the game of life, one of the most humiliating experiences is to foul out when the bases are loaded.

Life is but a brief lull between the stork and the epitaph.

LIQUOR

The only person who can handle a pint or a quart while driving is the milkman.

Any safety campaign that does not throttle booze overlooks the main cause of accidents and crime.

Too many people attempt to fight the battles of life with a bottle.

Drinking liquor will not drown sorrows; it only irrigates them.

Some people have a veneer that comes off easily with a little liquor.

Whiskey has more lovers and fewer friends than anything else on earth.

Many men give up drinking on account of the wife and bad kidneys.

Liquor is nothing but trouble put in liquid form.

Some battle their way to the top—others bottle their way to the bottom.

Liquor talks mighty loud when it gets loose from the bottle, jug or glass.

Booze increases business for the hospitals, ambulance drivers, doctors, nurses, undertakers, and grave-diggers.

Without his bank account the "problem drinker" would be called a "drunken bum."

LOVE

He who falls in love with himself will have no rivals.

Love quickens all the senses—except common sense.

The love of God cannot be merited or earned, but it can be spurned.

It would be a happier world if love were as easy to keep as it is to make.

The Bible admonishes us to love our neighbors, and also to love our enemies; probably because they are generally the same people.

Love at first sight is often cured by a second look.

It is extremely difficult to express love with a clenched fist.

Love is more easily demonstrated than defined.

One of the tragedies of American life is that love is being defined by those who have experienced but little of it.

Those who deserve love least, need it most.

Another good way for a young man to waste his breath is trying to be reasonable about love.

Love is something different from delirium, but it's hard to tell the difference.

The only doctor who can cure a young couple who is in love is a Doctor of Divinity.

Illicit love isn't much fun once it gets into court.

Love at first sight is very practical; think of the time and money it saves!

LUCK

Luck is what happens when preparation meets opportunity.

The harder you work, the luckier you get.

Good luck often has the odor of perspiration about it.

Depend on the rabbit's foot if you will, but remember it didn't work for the rabbit!

The only sure thing about luck is that it will change.

Luck is good planning, carefully executed.

If anything lucky happens to you, don't forget to tell your friends in order to annoy them.

There may be luck in getting a job—but there's no luck involved in keeping it.

Combine common sense and the Golden Rule and you will have very little bad luck.

Luck always seems to be against the man who depends on it.

M

MAN

History records only one indispensable man—Adam.

The average man doesn't want much and usually gets less than that.

An upright man can never be a downright failure.

The trouble with the self-made man is that he often quits the job too soon.

When a man says he is going to do this or that tomorrow, ask him what he did yesterday.

The most wonderful thing ever made by man is a living for his family.

Every man has his price so we are told, but some hold bargain sales.

The average man is 42 around the chest, 44 around the waist, 96 around the golf course, and a nuisance around the house.

Man starts life young and broke and winds up old an bent.

The average man thinks he isn't.

MARRIAGE

A mother who makes a match for her daughter usually intends to referee it as well.

A good many things are easier said than done—including the marriage ritual.

Something every couple should save for their old age is marriage.

Nothing makes a marriage rust like distrust.

The best things to get out of marriage are children.

A marriage may be a holy wedlock, or an unholy deadlock.

What marriage needs is more open minds and a lot fewer open mouths.

When a boy marries, his mother thinks he is throwing himself away, and his sisters think the girl is.

There is entirely too much worrying about unhappy marriages. All marriages are happy. It's only living together afterward that causes the trouble.

Marriage was formerly a contract, but now it is often regarded as a ninety-day option.

To marry a woman for her beauty is like buying a house for its paint.

Marriages are made in heaven—so are thunder and lightning.

MEMORY

A stroll down memory lane would be most pleasant if we could detour around a few "rough spots."

Among the things that enable a man to be self-satisifed is a poor memory.

Memory is the power to gather roses in January.

Some people remember a lie for ten years, but forget the truth in ten minutes.

A good memory test is to recall all the kind things you have said about your neighbor.

It's hard to remember way back when people would not buy things they couldn't pay for.

Creditors have better memories than debtors.

You must arrange in advance for pleasant memories.

Isn't it funny how some people can remember a joke, but can't seem to recall an unpaid bill?

Every time you lend money to a friend you damage his memory.

MIND

The person who doesn't know his own mind probably hasn't missed much.

Great minds discuss ideas, average minds discuss events, small minds discuss people.

The head never begins to swell until the mind stops growing.

Quite often when a man thinks his mind is getting broader—it is only his conscience stretching.

A lot of folks need to give their minds a bath.

Every "piece of your mind" you give another merely adds to your own vacuum.

A single-track mind is all right if it is on the right track.

Your stomach can be full but not your mind.

Some people seem to think a fertile mind requires a lot of dirt.

The human mind was intended for a storehouse, not a waste basket.

Some minds should be cultivated; others should be plowed under.

The most difficult thing to open is a closed mind.

Some minds are like concrete—thoroughly mixed and permanently set.

Great minds have purposes; others have wishes.

Instead of great minds being in the same channel, sometimes it's a matter of little minds being in the same rut.

Too many of us are broad-minded about the wrong things.

MISTAKES

To make a mistake is human, to repeat old mistakes is stupid.

Some people never make a mistake, nor do they ever make anything else.

A mistake is at least proof that some one was trying to accomplish something.

The man who invented the eraser had the human race pretty well sized-up.

If people learn from their mistakes, a lot of folks these days are getting a broad education.

The man who never makes an error never plays much ball.

When someone makes a mistake, rub it out, don't rub it in.

A man must be big enough to admit his mistakes, smart enough to profit from them, and strong enough to correct them.

The only thing most of us learn from our mistakes is to blame them on someone else.

When a fellow makes the same mistake twice, he's got to own up to carelessness or cussedness.

We make a big mistake putting silencers on guns and not on guitars.

The husband who brags that he never made a mistake has a wife who did.

MONEY

In the good old days, the man who saved money was a miser. Now, he's a wonder.

Some people get the idea they are worth a lot of money just because they have it.

When a man is broke, you can count his friends on his thumb.

These days about the only thing that's not enriched, fortified, or reinforced is money.

The love of money, and the lack of it, is the root of all kinds of evil.

Another reason you can't take it with you—it goes before you do.

If you want to know the value of money, try and borrow some.

Friendless indeed is the man who has friends only because he has money.

Money brings happiness to those who find happiness earning it.

We are told that money isn't everything. This may be true, but it's way ahead of whatever is in second place.

It's true that money talks, but nowadays you can't hold on to it long enough to start a conversation.

Money is a good servant, but a poor master.

MOTHER

A modern mother is one who can hold a safety pin and a cigarette in her mouth at the same time.

Simply having children does not necessarily make a woman a mother.

A typical mother is one who, seeing there are only four pieces of pie for five people, promptly announces she never did care for pie.

Throughout the ages no nation has ever had a better friend than the mother who taught her children to pray.

A mother takes 21 years to make a man of her boy, and another woman can make a fool of him in 20 minutes.

The most difficult thing for a mother to remember is that other people have perfect children, too.

Why does a mother do all she can to help her daughter catch a man—and then cry at her wedding?

The joys of motherhood are not fully experienced until all the children are in bed.

Many mothers in the last generation had their daughters vaccinated in places they wrongly thought would never show.

The role of a suburban mother is to deliver children: Obstetrically once, and by car forever.

MUSIC

An unsung hero is a guy who knows he can't sing and doesn't.

The musician who invented "swing" ought to.

It seems that songs making the most money make the least sense.

Now for a brief lesson in music: B-sharp; never B-flat; always B-natural.

Many a musician who plays Beethoven should play bridge.

There is plenty of heavenly music for those who are tuned in.

Musicians who play by ear should remember that people listen the same way.

Learning to play the saxophone should either improve the execution of the player or hasten it.

If today's music is a thing of beauty which will endure forever, the prospect of immortality is a dismal one.

There should be music in every home—except the one next door.

Nowadays, whatever is not worth saying is sung.

Opera is where a guy gets stabbed in the back, and instead of bleeding he sings.

A lot of singers on TV are worth watching. Too bad they're not worth listening to.

There's a place, no doubt, for jazz, but it sounds a little harsh to name it.

If you can write a song that's crazy enough, your fortune is made.

There's one advantage to the music the younger generation goes for today—nobody can whistle it.

What this country needs is more short-haired music.

A folk singer is a guy who sings through his nose by ear.

Today it isn't facing the music that hurts, it's listening to it.

Even if "Rock 'N' Roll" music died tomorrow, it would take five years for the sound to fade away.

You don't have to be much of a musician to toot your own horn.

N

NATURE

Nature makes blunders too. She often gives the biggest mouths to those who have the least to say.

It's a shame that Nature did not provide everyone with two additional senses—horse and common.

Nature didn't make us perfect, so she did the next best thing. She made us blind to our faults.

Human nature seems to endow every man with the ability to size up everybody but himself.

It's easier to understand human nature by bearing in mind that almost everybody thinks he's an exception to most rules.

Another mistake Nature sometimes makes: She often puts all the bones in the head and none in the back.

Nature never intended for us to pat ourselves on the back. If she had, our hinges would be different.

You can't change human nature, but perhaps you can improve it.

Nature must have a sense of humor to let spring fever and house cleaning come at the same time.

People who say that you cannot fool Nature have never watched a beauty shop operator work.

Nature often makes up for a nugget-size brain with a bucket-size mouth.

Man has now conquered almost every dangerous thing in nature except human nature.

NEIGHBORS

It's hard to keep up with the neighbors without falling behind with the creditors.

One record we are anxious to break is the one our neighbor plays around 1:00 in the morning.

A man cannot touch his neighbor's heart with anything less than his own.

Borrowing neighbors will take anything but a hint.

Neighbors resent hearing a married couple have words—especially when half of them can't be understood.

A neighbor is a person who is always doing something you can't afford to do.

The ideal neighbor is the one who makes his noise at the same time you make yours.

Your neighbor will seem like a better man when you judge him as you judge yourself.

Nothing makes you more tolerant of a neighbor's noisy party than being invited to it.

A good neighbor is a fellow who smiles at you over the back fence but doesn't climb it.

NEW YEAR

The New Year is somewhat like a new baby—many changes will be necessary, some of which may be neglected.

What the New Year brings us will depend a great deal on what we bring to the New Year.

The New Year usually gives people a fresh start on their old habits.

New Year is when some folks drop in for a call and others call in for a drop.

O

OLD AGE

The worst thing about growing old is having to listen to a lot of advice from one's children.

It's funny how we never get too old to learn some new way to be foolish.

Three things indicate we are getting old. First, there is a loss of memory—and we can't remember the other two.

Don't resent growing old—many are denied the privilege.

One of the nice things of old age is that you can whistle while you brush your teeth.

It is magnificent to grow old, if one keeps young.

By the time old people decide it is wise to watch their step they aren't going anywhere.

Old age is something that everybody else reaches before we do.

Nowadays, most women grow old gracefully; most men, disgracefully.

One of the special privileges of old age is to relate experiences that nobody will believe, and give advice that nobody will follow.

The principal objection to old age is that there's no future in it.

Some people will never live to be as old as they look.

About the best way to grow old is not to be in too much of a hurry about it.

Growing old is no cause for hysteria. The rose bush does not scream when the petals begin to fall.

Old age is that time of life when you don't care where your wife goes, just so you don't have to go with her.

When saving for old age, be sure to lay up a few pleasant thoughts.

The only way to keep from growing old is to die young.

About the best thing concerning old age is that a fellow doesn't have to go through it but once.

You're really getting old if, on arising in the morning, you have to decide whether to put on your glasses or put in your teeth.

OPINIONS

An obstinate man does not hold opinions—they hold him.

A man's opinions often change, except the one he has of himself.

You can't keep folks from having a bad opinion of you, but you can keep them from being right about it.

The man who has strong opinions and says what he thinks is courageous—and friendless.

It's a lot easier to form an opinion when you don't have all the facts.

An opinion is a prejudice with a few unrelated facts.

Public opinion is the greatest force for good—when it happens to be on that side.

Everyone has the right to express an opinion, however no one has the right to expect everyone to listen.

The quickest way to kindle a fire is to rub two opposing opinions together.

A wise man generally gives other people's opinion about as much weight as he does his own.

Popular opinion is generally based upon prejudice and ignorance.

About the only opinions that do not eventually change are the ones we have about ourselves.

OPPORTUNITY

The reason a lot of people cannot find opportunity is that it goes around disguised as hard work.

You don't have to be in a key position to open the door of opportunity.

Opportunity is often missed because we are broadcasting when we should be listening.

Why don't we jump at opportunities as quickly as we jump to conclusions?

No opportunity is ever lost. The other fellow takes those we miss.

How much better this world would be if we would let opportunity do all the knocking.

Life is full of hard knocks, but answer them all. One might be opportunity.

God makes opportunities, but He expects us to hunt for them.

Seize opportunity as it comes and you won't have to chase it after it goes by.

Never neglect the opportunity of keeping your mouth shut.

Even when opportunity knocks, a man still has to get up off his seat and open the door.

You may find much that you have lost, but never a lost opportunity.

A great opportunity will only make you look ridiculous unless you are prepared to meet it.

When you have a chance to embrace an opportunity, give it a big hug.

OUR NEEDS

What our country needs is a good five-cent anything.

Man's greatest need is something to feel important about.

Another great need of this country is guns of smaller and men of larger caliber.

The greatest need of this generation is fewer automobile drivers and more wheelbarrow pushers.

Our country's most basic needs can be summed up in four words, bread, brains, beliefs, and brotherhood.

This country needs a man who can be right and president at the same time.

The crying need of this country is less public speaking and more private thinking.

What America needs is a return to Saturday night baths and Sunday morning church going.

Above all things, we need tranquility without tranquilizers.

We stand greatly in need of a good silent electric guitar.

America needs more free speech that is worth listening to.

P

PARENTS

Too many parents tie up their dogs and let their children run loose.

Why do some parents TAKE their children to the circus but SEND them to Sunday School?

The best thing parents can spend on their children is time—not money.

Give American parents credit—they know how to obey their children.

Parents are people who bear infants, bore teen-agers, and board newly-weds.

Nothing worries a parent more than the uneasy feeling that his children are relying more on his example than his advice.

The ability to say NO is perhaps the greatest gift a parent has.

Some parents really bring their children up, others let them down.

The frightening thing about heredity and environment is that parents provide both.

Parents would not have to worry so much about how a kid turns out if they worried more about when he turns in.

Did you hear about the father who fainted when his son asked for the keys to the garage and came out with the lawn mower?

The accent may be on youth these days, but the stress is still on the parents.

It is beginning to look like America has too many part-time parents.

Some parents begin with giving in and end with giving up.

All a parent has to do to make a child thirsty is to fall asleep.

Parenthood is a gamble. You never know how far you're going to be driven out of your mind.

The modern father wants his son to have all the things he never had—such as straight A's on his report card.

Parents who make a career out of sticking to close family ties seldom see these relations come unglued.

PATIENCE

Patience is the ability to throttle your motor when you feel like stripping the gears.

Wait patiently and sooner or later something will turn up—your nose, your toes, or both.

This would be a wonderful world if men showed as much patience in all things as they do in waiting for a fish to bite.

You should bear with people because people have to bear with you.

Patience is the ability to stand something as long as it happens to the other fellow.

Lack of pep is often mistaken for patience.

It is easy finding reasons why other folks should be patient.

Patience is a quality that is most needed when it is exhausted.

The secret of patience is doing something else in the meantime.

A mother's patience is like a tube of toothpaste—it's never quite all gone.

The trouble with patience is the more a fellow has, the more folks want to use it.

Everything we have is taxed—even our patience.

Many a man has turned and left the dock just before his ship came in.

Patience is when you listen silently to someone else tell about the same operation you had.

Even a waiter finally comes to him who waits.

The trouble with people today is that they want to get to the promised land without going through the wilderness.

PEACE

Peace is a period of international truce when haggling and cheating replace fighting.

Peace is a thing you can't have by throwing rocks at a hornet's nest.

What the world needs is the peace that passes all misunderstanding.

There will be no peace as long as God remains unseated at the conference table.

The dove of peace still finds the world covered with the waters of hate and jealousy.

Peace won by compromise is a short-lived achievement.

It's mighty hard to find everlasting peace as long as there are more dogs than bones.

Perpetual peace seems as far removed as perpetual motion.

When a man finds no peace within himself, it is useless to seek it elsewhere.

Thousands of Americans are trying to find peace in a pill.

Peace is not made in documents, but in the hearts of men.

Another argument in favor of a lasting peace is that it would give us time to finish paying for the last war.

Peace is a period of confusion and unrest between wars.

Even peace may be purchased at too high a price.

It pays to preserve your peace of mind. It's the only peace you can find.

There can be no peace in the world until the caliber of its statesmen are equal to the caliber of its guns.

Keeping peace in a large family requires patience, love, understanding and at least two television sets.

Everybody seems to smoke the pipe of peace—but very few inhale.

There's just one sure way to find peace—look at it in the dictionary.

Another thing that keeps police busy is breaking up fights at peace rallies.

PEOPLE

There are two things some people never seem to get—all they want and all they deserve.

A lot of people consider themselves ahead of the times when they aren't even going in the same direction.

Many people never know where the next check is coming from or when the last one is coming back.

If some people preached what they practice, it would have to be censored.

No two people are alike and both of them are glad of it.

People will fight for everything that's coming to them—whether they want it or not.

Quiet people aren't the only ones who don't say much.

People generally look too high for things close by.

There are some people who can't tell a lie, some who can't tell the truth, and a few others who can't tell the difference.

It is real nice that some people take all the blame for being self-made.

The only thing some people can keep in their heads overnight is a cold.

Nothing is something many people are good for.

Some people think they are bearing their cross when they're only putting up with themselves.

There are a few people who are like boats—they toot loudest when in a fog.

You can't tell if some people are the strong, silent type or just dumb.

People are certainly funny—they want to be in the front of the bus, in the back of the church, and in the middle of the road.

People who do the most for the world's advancement are the ones who demand the least.

The trouble with many people is they stop faster than they start.

We are told that there can be no vacuum, but lots of people come close. Some people are like wheelbarrows, trailers or canoes. They need to be pushed, pulled or paddled.

PERFECTION

If biologists are right in their assertion that there is not a perfect man on earth today, a lot of personal opinions here and there will have to be altered.

The nearest to perfection that most people ever come is when filling out an employment application.

We all know it isn't human to be perfect and too many of us take advantage of it.

A man who knows his imperfections is just about as perfect as it is possible for anyone to be.

If you wish to be perfect, follow the advice that you give to others.

A perfectionist is one who takes great pains—and gives them to others.

The only thing that even approaches perfection in this world is an alarm clock that doesn't ring.

PESSIMISTS

A pessimist can hardly wait for the future so he can look back with regret.

A pessimist thinks the world is against him—and it is.

Most all pessimists are seasick during the entire voyage of their lives.

A pessimist has no motor; an optimist has no brakes.

A pessimist, when he has the choice of two evils, takes both.

A pessimist doesn't expect to get anything on a silver platter but tarnish.

For some reason, a pessimist always complains of the noise when opportunity knocks.

When a pessimist sizes himself up, he always gets sore about it.

A pessimist is the best person to borrow from. He never expects to get it back.

If it were not for the optimist, the pessimist would never know how happy he isn't.

POPULARITY

Your popularity will depend on HOW you treat your friends—and how often.

The man of the hour spent many days and nights getting there.

Popularity is a matter of whether people like you wherever you go or like it whenever you leave.

If you want to be popular, keep your ears open, and most of the time your mouth shut.

Popularity is a form of success that's seldom worth the things we have to do in order to attain it.

One way to be popular is to listen attentively to a lot of things you already know.

POVERTY

Poverty is no disgrace, but that's about all one can say in its favor.

Being poor is a problem, but being rich isn't always the answer.

It's a toss-up whether it is worse to be old and bent or young and broke.

When you hear a man say that poverty is a great thing for the character, the chances are that you're listening to a millionaire.

The real tragedy of the poor is that they can't afford anything but self-denial.

Poverty is a state of existence which deprives a person of many things he is better off without.

The easiest way to remain poor is to pretend to be rich.

Poverty of purpose is worse than poverty of purse.

Some men were broke when they got married, and have held their own ever since.

The poorest of all men is not the one without a cent. It's the man without a dream.

There's one advantage of being poor—the doctor will cure you faster.

When we're poor we try to hide it, but in our memoirs we brag about it.

Poverty isn't dishonorable in itself—but it is dishonorable when it comes from idleness, intemperance, extravagance and folly.

For many, the idea of poverty is black-and-white television.

Poverty has its drawbacks, but it has enabled many a man to have a good reputation that he wouldn't have had if he had been wealthy.

One good thing about being poor, it's inexpensive.

"Poverty is a state of mind," says the philosopher with a full stomach.

There is one thing about poverty—it sticks to a fellow even after most of his friends leave him.

PRAYER

Live prayerfully, the life you save may be your own.

Prayer must mean something to us if it is to mean anything to God.

If you must talk—why not pray?

Prayer will either make a man leave off sinning, or sin will make him leave off prayer.

A lot of little prayers as we go along through life would save a long one in case of emergency.

If you must tell God HOW to lead, why not just go ahead yourself?

A young Christian once prayed as follows, "Lord, fill me to overflowing. I can't hold much, but I can overflow a great deal."

Prayer does not need proof; it needs practice.

You cannot stumble if you are on your knees.

If you are too busy to pray, you are too busy.

Sooner or later we all need some foreign aid—the kind we get from praying.

A short prayer will reach the Throne of Grace—if you don't live too far away.

Prayer can't be taken out of the public schools. That's the way, the only way, many of us got through.

Some people feel we don't need prayer any more since we now have penicillin.

A lot of kneeling keeps you in good standing with God.

Prayer by people in the pew will give the preacher power in the pulpit.

The prayers a man lives on his feet are just as important as those he says on his knees.

Too many of us are like the old deacon who prayed, "Use me, O Lord, in thy work—especially in an advisory capacity."

Nothing lies outside the reach of prayer except that which is outside the will of God.

If you would have God hear you when you pray, you must hear Him when He speaks.

PREACHERS

If, in his sermon, the preacher aims at nothing, he usually hits it.

A preacher's pious look will not cover a poorly prepared sermon.

When some preachers get up, their thoughts sit down.

Second wind is what some preachers get when they say, "And now in conclusion."

Preachers don't talk in their sleep; they talk in other people's sleep.

A preacher who wants to make a big noise should get a job in a boiler factory.

Don't pack the preacher in an ice house all year and then abuse him if he doesn't sweat.

All preachers should be sure of what they are saying. Some one in the audience might be listening.

The preacher always does his poorest shooting when he allows others to load him.

Preachers find more sleeping sickness than does the physician.

Jonah learned more at the bottom of the sea than some preachers learn at a theological seminary.

The world looks at preachers out of the pulpit to know what they mean in it.

A preacher usually takes a text and preaches from it—sometimes very far from it.

Far too many preachers, when they get into the pulpit, are dealers in dry goods and notions.

If there is no hell, many preachers are obtaining money under false pretense.

Some preachers are so sad of voice and countenance that they should apply for membership in the embalmers union.

A popular preacher is one who knows when to draw the line between preaching and meddling.

Some preachers seem to use big words to conceal the smallness of their thoughts.

Preachers are determined—if they don't get on your toes they get in your hair.

Just before immersing the candidate, the preacher remarked, "I hope I have a tither in the tank."

PREJUDICE

Prejudice is a great time-saver. It enables one to form opinions without bothering to get the facts.

The judgment of a man on a subject on which he is prejudiced isn't really worth much.

Prejudice is a lazy man's substitute for thinking.

A great many people think they are thinking when they are merely rearranging their prejudices.

No prejudice has ever been able to prove its case in the court of reason.

Prejudice usually squints when it looks and lies when it talks.

Don't air your prejudices; smother them.

Prejudice is when you decide some fellow is a stinker before you even meet him.

It isn't easy for an idea to squeeze its way into a head that is filled with prejudice.

Prejudice is a loose idea tightly held.

PROBLEMS

Man's biggest problem is not "outer space" but "inner space."

Never before has the world had so many big problems and so many little minds.

The trouble with today's problems is that we can't turn to the back of the book for the answers.

If you can't state your problem in ten words or less, you don't understand it yourself.

Problems shouldn't be faced; they should be attacked.

Why can't life's problems hit us when we are 18 and know everything?

The problems of the world are changing so fast that some of them become obsolete before they can cause any real trouble.

There is no perfect solution to any problem that's got human beings mixed up in it.

The reason some people know the solution is because they created the problem.

Psychiatrists tell us that talking helps to solve problems—it causes them, too.

If you could kick the fellow responsible for most of your problems you couldn't sit down for two months.

A problem not worth praying about is not worth worrying about.

PROSPERITY

In prosperous times a lot of folks are better off than they are better.

Only Americans have mastered the art of being prosperous though broke.

Few of us can stand prosperity—especially of the other fellow.

No one has ever backed into prosperity.

Until he becomes prosperous, a man doesn't realize how many old friends he has.

It may be true that most people can't stand prosperity. But it's also true that most people don't have to.

You can always tell when an American is prosperous because he fills his home with old furniture and new whiskey.

Prosperous times are when you pay installments on ten things instead of one.

Prosperity seems to be skidding just a bit coming around the corner.

Sometimes virtue and prosperity have trouble living together.

In prosperity men ask too little of God. In adversity, too much.

Prosperity often means it is just a matter of not being quite as broke this month as last month.

Never before in our history has America's horn of plenty had such a toot.

When prosperity comes, don't use all of it.

Q

QUESTIONS

You can usually dodge a question with a long-winded answer.

Seems like that when we know the right answers no one asks us the right questions.

It is not every question that deserves an answer.

Beware of the man who knows the answer before he understands the question!

There are two sides to every question except when it happens to be a love triangle.

If there are always two sides to every question, how come there's only one answer?

The paramount question before the country today is, "How much is the down payment?"

It is always easier to see both sides of a question if your prejudices or money aren't involved.

Most of us are sufficiently broadminded to admit that there are two sides to every question—our own side, and the side that no intelligent, informed, sane and self-respecting citizen could possibly hold.

What is more embarrassing than to ask a 30-cent question and have to listen to a 64-dollar answer?

R

RELIGION

Some people really enjoy their religion, others just endure it.

Religion costs, but irreligion costs more.

It is never worthwhile to argue about the religion you don't have.

A bitter world cannot be sweetened by a sour religion.

Very often a person who boasts of having no religious prejudice has no religion either.

Why expect men to unite on religion when they can't on anything else?

Too many folks use their religion as they do a bus, they ride it only when it is going their way.

Religion is meant to be bread for daily use, not cake for special occasions.

Men will wrangle for religion, write for it, die for it; anything but live for it.

Many people lose their religion by letting it escape through their mouth.

If the people were as religious as statistics show them to be we could get along fine with fewer police.

Religion is no different from other things. The less you invest in it, the poorer its quality.

The fellow who argues that all religions should unite probably doesn't speak to his own brother-in-law.

Too many people are interested in a religion that makes them look good without having to act that way.

Religion is like music, it does not need defense, but rendition.

Some people think that all the equipment you need to discuss religion is a mouth.

If people are so wicked with religion as some contend, what would they be without it?

The religion that makes you feel like fighting your brother never came from your Father.

People seldom lose their religion by a blowout, usually it's just a slow leak.

A magazine writer says we need a new religion. But let's not do anything rash until we try the old one.

Most people have some sort of religion; at least they know what church they're staying away from.

A religion that does nothing, costs nothing, suffers nothing—is worth nothing.

There are still a few people who think that religion is like a faucet; to be turned on and off as the need presents itself.

You cannot prove your religion by its noise.

What a fine world this would be if people would spend as much energy practicing their religion as they spend quarreling about it.

A religion that won't take you to church services certainly won't take you to heaven.

The religion of many men is in their wife's name.

Religion is a cloak used by some people in this world who will be warm enough without one in the next.

If you have no joy in your religion, there's a leak in your Christianity somewhere.

Arguing about religion is much easier than practicing it.

It's time for us to stop putting more saints in stained glass and start putting more in shoe leather.

More time in God's house will bring better times in our house.

REPENTANCE

To grieve over sin is one thing; to repent is another.

You can't repent too soon because you do not know how soon it may be too late.

Some people repent of their sins by thanking the Lord they aren't half as bad as some of their neighbors.

Did you ever feel that some people who often repent loud and long are really just bragging?

True repentance has a double aspect; it looks upon things past with a weeping eye, and upon the future with a watchful eye.

We can easily repent of the sins we've committed in the past, but how about those we intend to commit in the future?

A few people have been known to become so religious while dying that they actually repented of sins which they had never committed.

REPUTATION

Reputation is one of the few things that looks worse when you try to decorate it.

Many a man gets a reputation for being energetic when in truth he is merely fidgety.

What people say to your back is your standing in the community.

You can trust any number of people with your money, but very few with your reputation.

There are plenty of people in the world with good reputations who have never been found out.

The easiest thing to get but the most difficult thing to get rid of is a bad reputation.

It is easier to acquire a good reputation than to lose a bad one.

A good reputation, like good will, is built up by many actions, and may be lost by one.

Nothing deflates as fast as a punctured reputation.

Many a man's reputation would not recognize his character if they met in the dark.

You have to be quite a juggler if you have a reputation to keep up and one to live down.

Reputation is a large bubble which bursts when you try to blow it up yourself.

If some folks lost their reputation they would be lucky.

RESPONSIBILITY

Some people grow under responsibility, while others only swell.

Those who shrink from responsibilities keep on shrinking in other ways, too.

If you want to keep your feet on the ground, carry some responsibilities on your shoulders.

If the responsibility for all poverty is placed upon the wealthy, why not blame all sickness on the healthy?

When you take responsibilities on your shoulders there is not much room left for chips.

It is easy to dodge our responsibilities but we cannot dodge the consequences of dodging our responsibilities.

Responsibility develops some men and ruins others.

We are not responsible for many of the things that happen to us, but we are responsible for the way we react when they do happen.

REVENGE

Revenge may be sweet, but not when you are on the receiving end.

There is no passion of the human heart that promises so much and pays so little as that of revenge.

Revenge is the poorest victory in all the world. To kill a hornet after he has strung you never was known to make the wound heal any faster.

Many people are willing to give you a cup of cold water if they can only get it down the back of your neck.

Revenge is often like you biting a dog because the dog bites you.

If revenge is sweet, why does it leave such a bitter taste?

RICHES

If you would like to get rich, earn a little more than you spend—and keep on doing it.

Just pretending to be rich keeps some people poor.

No amount of riches can atone for poverty of character.

Anybody could get rich if he could guess the exact moment at which a piece of junk becomes an antique.

It's extremely difficult for a rich man to enter the kingdom of heaven, but it's not difficult for him to get on the church board of trustees.

The rich may not live longer, but it certainly seems like it to their poor relatives.

No man is rich enough to buy back his past.

Whatever it is that keeps people from getting rich—most of us have it.

Riches are a golden key that opens every door save that of heaven.

Plenty in the purse cannot prevent starvation in the soul.

Fewer folks nowadays are suffering from the embarrassment of riches.

It is about as hard for a rich man to enter heaven as it is for a poor man to remain on earth.

The futility of riches is stated very plainly in two places; the Bible and the income tax form.

RIGHTEOUSNESS

There are only two classes of people: The righteous and the unrighteous. The classifying is always done by the righteous.

Garments of righteousness never go out of style.

Where there is no thirst for righteousness, the sermon is always "dry."

Righteousness does not consist in being just a little less bad than our neighbors.

Even the hypocrite admires righteousness. That is why he imitates it.

You can always tell when you are on the road of righteousness—it's uphill.

RIGHT LIVING

No man ever got lost on a straight road.

He who walks circumspectly by day need not fear the rap on the door at midnight.

Always do right; it will gratify some people and astonish others.

Be careful how you live. You may be the only Bible some people will ever read.

There is never any traffic congestion on the straight and narrow road.

What a fine world this would be if today we did as well as we expect to do tomorrow.

A lot of people would do right if they thought it was wrong.

So live that people will want your autograph and not your fingerprints.

The only way to be good is to obey God, love your fellow man, and hate the devil.

Live each day so you will neither be afraid of tomorrow nor ashamed of yesterday.

Be on the level and you are not likely to go downhill.

Straight living cannot come out of crooked thinking.

Always stand for the right; then you win if you lose.

No man can be at peace with God without getting into an argument with the devil.

If people generally cared for their souls as they do their looks, the preachers would soon be out of a job.

Remember your spiritual system, forget your nervous system, and you'll have a place in God's heavenly system.

An upright man can never be a downright failure.

Live your life so that you won't be afraid to have your phone tapped.

It is better to be beaten in the right than to succeed in the wrong.

The straight and narrow road has not yet developed enough traffic to require a four-lane highway.

So live that when the preacher has ended his remarks, those present will not think they have attended the wrong funeral.

Right living is better than high living—and cheaper.

RUMORS

There are no idle rumors. They are all busy.

A rumor is about as hard to unspread as butter.

As yet, no one has invented a self-starting rumor.

It is easier to float a rumor than to sink one.

All rumors should be fitted with girdles to keep them from spreading.

There is nothing busier than a so-called idle rumor.

Some people will believe anything, if you tell them it's a rumor.

A rumor is like a check—never endorse it till you're sure its genuine.

We still can't understand how rumors without a leg to stand on get around so fast.

A lot of people seem to have "Rumor-tism."

S

SCANDALS

A scandal is one thing that has to be bad to be good.

Usually the half that has not been told is the better half.

A scandal is the art of saying nothing in such a way that leaves practically nothing unsaid.

The trouble about a skeleton in a closet is that it does not have sense enough to stay there.

A scandal is somewhat like an egg; when it is hatched it has wings.

A breath of scandal makes conversation breezy for some people.

A scandal is what half the world takes pleasure in inventing and the other half in believing.

SELF-CONTROL

What chance can a man have to control his destiny when he cannot control himself?

Self-expression is good; self-control is better.

Self-control might be defined as the ability to carry a credit card and not abuse it.

At no time is self-control more difficult than in times of success.

Had you ever noticed that self-control comes in mighty handy when eating salted peanuts?

Self-control is giving up smoking cigarettes; extreme self-control is not telling anybody about it.

SELFISHNESS

It's give and take in this world, with too many people trying to take.

Of course there are a few selfish people here and there—mostly there.

He who lives for himself does not have very much to live for.

Selfishness is that detestable vice which no one will tolerate in others and no one is without in himself.

One who cares only for himself when young will be stingy in middle-age, and a wretched miser in old age.

There's no promise of heavenly reward to the man who gives away an old overcoat in August.

Selfishness tarnishes everything it touches.

A man who lives for himself is ruined by the company he keeps.

The person who lives for self alone usually dies the same way.

115

Selfishness short-circuits prayer.

The man who lives only for himself runs a very small business.

SERMONS

The best test of a sermon is depth, not length.

Everybody should listen to a sermon occasionally, including those who go to church.

Many sermons are dull because preachers often try to answer questions that nobody is asking.

The world today is hearing too many sermons and seeing too few.

Preachers should learn that for a sermon to be immortal, it need not be eternal.

The sermon will be better if you listen to it as a Christian rather than a critic.

If a sermon pricks the conscience, it must have good points.

The old-fashioned sermon on hell wasn't so different from the ones we hear today on current events.

Many preachers, in preparing their sermons, prepare no place to stop.

Before passing judgment on a sermon be sure to try it out in practice.

It is easier to preach ten sermons than it is to live one.

How can a preacher expect to fill heaven with people when his sermons won't even fill the church building where he preaches?

If some sermons don't reach down to posterity, it won't be due to the fact they aren't long enough.

A good sermon should be preached over and over. A bad one ought not to be preached at all.

The best way to compliment the sermon delivered by your minister is to bring a friend to hear the next one.

There are very few souls saved after the first twenty-five minutes of a sermon.

A man usually considers it a good sermon when he feels that the preacher didn't refer directly to him.

If, before criticizing the sermon, why not consider how much it actually cost you? You might conclude that you got your money's worth.

The eternal gospel does not require an everlasting sermon.

In case of people falling asleep during the sermon, the preacher needs waking up.

A good sermon helps in two ways. Some rise from it greatly strengthened. Others wake from it refreshed.

Some sermons are a mile long and two inches deep.

You can find the world's shortest sermon on a traffic sign, "Keep Right."

A great many sermons are of the cotton candy variety: Colorful, sweet, harmless, and a bit short on content.

Very few people find a sermon long if it is helpful.

We've become so keyed-up and nervous that it is now almost impossible to put people to sleep with a sermon.

Every sermon should change the person in the pew, or it should be changed by the preacher in the pulpit.

Some people think a thirty-minute sermon is too long, so they substitute a three hundred column Sunday newspaper.

A sermon should never be preached until it has been soaked in prayer.

Too many people would rather hear a good sermon on Sunday than live one through the week.

A good sermon should not only comfort the afflicted—but also afflict the comfortable.

It's easy to appreciate the points of a sermon that prods the other fellow.

One of the best things about sermons is the ease with which we can listen to them while thinking about something entirely different.

You can preach a better sermon with your life than with your lips.

SILENCE

You can learn a lot about a man by how much he doesn't say.

Don't repeat anything you will not sign your name to.

Another nice thing about silence is that it can't be repeated.

To avoid trouble and insure safety, breathe through your nose. It keeps the mouth shut.

Most of us know how to say nothing; few of us know when.

If men talked only about what they understand, the silence would become unbearable.

117

People who can hold their tongues rarely have any trouble holding their friends.

He who will not understand your silence will probably not understand your words.

A wise man, even when he is silent, says more than a fool when he talks.

When at a loss for the right word to say—try silence.

Keeping one's mouth shut keeps a lot of ignorance from leaking out.

Many a man who can't talk much makes a big hit keeping still.

Wise men are not always silent but they know when to be.

If a thing will go without saying—let it.

Blessed is the man who does not speak until he knows what he is talking about.

Some people we know should be wired for silence.

The art of silence is as great as that of speech.

No flies ever get into a shut mouth.

Very seldom can you improve on saying nothing.

If you don't say anything, you won't be called upon to repeat it.

SIN

There is always more sin when folks can afford it.

Our government could raise unlimited revenue simply by taxing sin.

Vice of any kind must become respectable before it is dangerous.

The wages of sin are always paid right on time.

Original sin is a misnomer because every kind of sin has been practiced before.

No matter how many new translations of the Bible are made, the people still sin the same way.

God may forgive your sins, but your nervous system won't.

Some men think they are saints because they are selective in their sins.

The three greatest sins of today are: Indifference to, neglect of, and disrespect for, the word of God.

Secret sins won't stay secret for very long.

Sin causes the cup of joy to spring a leak.

The unpardonable sin is for a person of a different race or religion from ours to be smarter than we are.

Inflation has affected everything except the wages of sin.

One reason why the way of the transgressor is so hard is because it's so crowded.

There may be some new sinners today, but there are no new sins.

No power on earth can make a man sin without his consent.

Sin would have very few takers if its consequences occurred immediately.

Some people think the sins of omission are the sins we ought to commit but don't.

Sin always starts out being fun.

The way of the transgressor may be hard—but it isn't lonely.

Sin is not inherited, but it is contagious.

Since most sins are quite expensive, it looks like folks would behave themselves and save the difference.

If and when the wages of sin are ever paid, a lot of people are going to get time and a half for overtime.

Unless sin is confessed it will fester.

A sin was once called a sin; now it's called a complex.

No man ever found the pleasure of sin like the picture of sin.

If you would not fall into sin, keep away from the brink of temptation.

A sin takes on new and real terrors when there seems to be a chance that it is going to be found out.

The wages of sin are the only wages not subject to the income tax.

Sin deceives, then defiles, then deadens.

One cannot be isolated from sin, but he can become insulated against it.

Some people are willing to do anything to become a Christian except to give up their sins.

The way of the transgressor is hard—especially on other people.

Confess your sins, not your neighbor's.

Making a sin legal does not make it harmless.

SUCCESS

Success is somewhat like falling off a log; you can't always explain exactly how it happened.

If at first you don't succeed—you're running about average.

No one has ever yet climbed the ladder of success with his hands in his pockets.

Success is the ability to get along with some people, and ahead of others.

The dictionary is the only place where success comes before work.

One of the biggest troubles with success is that its recipe is often the same as that for a nervous breakdown.

To succeed, you must be easy to start and hard to stop.

Success is the only thing some people cannot forgive in a friend.

Some people succeed because they find greener pastures; others, because they find greener people.

The most difficult part of getting to the top of the ladder is getting through the crowd at the bottom.

God gave to man five senses: Touch, taste, smell, sight, and hearing. The successful man has two more—horse and common.

There isn't any map on the road to success. You have to find your own way.

He has achieved success who has lived long, laughed often, and loved much.

A person interrupts and endangers his climb up the ladder of success when he stops to pat himself on the back.

The secret of success is still a secret to the average American.

There may be splinters in the ladder of success, but you don't notice them until you start sliding down.

Formula for success: When you start a thing, finish it.

The successful man has a wife who tells him what to do, and a secretary who does it.

Success is sweet, but its secret is sweat.

We would all be successful if we followed the advice we give to others.

T

TALKATIVENESS

Some people talk for hours without mentioning what they are talking about.

Listen carefully to some talkers and you will then know that practice does not make perfect.

Talk is cheap because the supply always exceeds the demand.

It seems that some folks turn their tongues on and leave them running.

Usually the first screw that gets loose in a person's head is the one that controls the tongue.

Did you ever notice how often a narrow mind and a wide mouth go together?

It isn't the people who tell all they know that causes most of the trouble in this world—it's the ones who tell more.

If there were forty-nine ways of talking without saying anything, some people know all of them.

Some talk wouldn't be so irritating if it weren't handed out in such large quantities.

The trouble with this country is that there are too many wide open spaces entirely surrounded by teeth.

A lot of people who talk constantly about capital and labor never had any capital and never did any labor.

Everybody wants to talk, few want to think, and nobody wants to listen.

A great many folks get the idea they are breezy when in reality they are only windy.

Don't use a gallon of words to express a spoonful of thought.

The unhappiest man is the one whose expenditure of speech is too great for his income of ideas.

Talking too much usually follows thinking too little.

Instead of broadcasting so much, why not try tuning in at intervals?

The mouths of many people seem to have the habit of going on active duty while their brains are on furlough!

What a wonderful world this would be if we all would think as much as we talk!

Some people are such talkers that you can't get a word in edgewise even if you folded it.

TEEN-AGERS

The most difficult job teen-agers have these days is learning good manners without seeing any.

Too many teen-agers don't pay any more attention to their conscience than they do their parents.

Teen-agers haven't changed much. They still grow up, leave home, and get married. The big difference is that today they don't always do it in that order.

Not only are teen-agers a comfort in old age—they help bring it on.

Little wonder that our present-day teen-ager is all mixed up. Half the adults are telling him to "find himself" and the other half is telling him to "get lost."

Perhaps the reason why teen-agers know all the answers is that they haven't heard all the questions yet.

The average teen-ager still has all the faults his parents outgrew.

Like its politicians and its wars, society has the teen-agers it deserves.

Once a teen-ager passes his driving test he can pass everything except his school subjects.

Did you hear about the teen-age boy who let his hair down—and smothered?

Teen-agers aren't interested in putting their shoulders to the wheel these days—all they want to do is get their hands on it.

A recent survey shows that the average teen-agers around the country are alike in many disrespects.

No one could possibly know as much as a teen-ager thinks he does or as little as he thinks his father knows.

122

The main trouble with teen-agers is that they're just like their parents were at their age.

Anyone who doesn't believe the younger generation is creative should watch a teen-ager construct a sandwich.

TEMPER

Your temper is a funny thing. You can't get rid of it by losing it.

Hitting the ceiling is the wrong way to get up in this world.

It is always a good idea to be selfish with your temper—so always keep it.

Temper is a gift which improves with non-use.

Men are like steel. When they lose their tempers they are worthless.

You can't cool the engine of your car by stripping the gears.

Striking while the iron is hot is all right, but don't strike while the head is hot.

Every time you give someone a piece of your mind you make your head a little emptier.

A show of temper is often a testimonial of indecision, weakness, inadequacy, defeat and frustration.

When a man loses his temper his reason goes on a vacation.

Temper shows most when it is lost.

A temper displayed in public is indecent exposure.

He who "blows his stack" adds to the world's pollution.

Before you give somebody a piece of your mind, be sure you can get by with what you have left.

TEMPTATION

Temptations are certain to ring your doorbell; but it's your own fault if you ask them in to stay for dinner.

When you meet temptation—turn to the right.

Most people who flee from temptation usually leave a forwarding address.

Temptations from without have no power unless there is corresponding desire within.

There are a lot of people who can resist everything except temptation.

Temptations are like tramps. Treat them kindly and they will return bringing others with them.

The man who is suddenly overpowered by temptation has probably been dreaming about it for a long time.

Watch out for temptation—the more you see it, the better it looks.

Man has more temptations than a woman mostly because he knows where to find them.

Most people don't need to be led into temptation—they usually find their own way.

By yielding to temptation one may lose in a moment what it took him a lifetime to gain.

Few speed records are broken when people run away from temptation.

Many of the world's most attractive temptations are like some television commercials: frequently deceptive, and frightfully costly.

Temptation usually comes in through a door that has deliberately been left open.

When temptation knocks, imagination usually answers.

Most of us keep one eye on the temptation we pray not to be led into.

Temptation is something, if resisted, may never come your way again.

Don't worry about avoiding temptation after you pass 60. That's when it starts avoiding you.

THINKING

When you stop to think, don't forget to start again.

People who say what they think would not be so bad if they thought.

There is entirely too much thinking these days by those who are not qualified to think.

We don't all think alike. In fact, we don't all think.

Which needs to be raised more—our standard of living or our standard of thinking?

The man who thinks he cannot is usually right.

Thinking is only a process of talking to yourself intelligently.

The trouble with most people is that every time they think, they think of themselves.

Serious thinking is the kind of thinking to which most people resort only when they're broke, in jail, in the hospital, or in some other disaster.

Five percent of the people really think, 10 percent think they think, and the remainder would rather die than think. It's the 5 percent that changes things.

Thinking is like loving and dying. Each of us must do it for himself.

Some people don't think before they speak—nor afterwards.

You can think better if you close your eyes—and your mouth.

There is a lingering suspicion on the part of some that the trouble with this country is that too many people are trying to think without having had any previous experience.

Some people can't think and the rest don't.

It is about time for folks to carry this do-it-yourself craze to thinking.

If it's true that people think best on their feet, there must be a lot of folks sitting around these days.

Some who make a habit of thinking out loud make others appreciate how golden silence really is.

Acting without thinking is like shooting without aiming.

Think small and you'll remain small.

THRIFT

Is thrift becoming unfashionable or just impossible?

The person who works and saves will someday have enough to divide with those who don't.

Thrift is a form of economy that generally limits its contributions to good advice.

Everybody thinks thrift is a wonderful virtue—especially in our ancestors.

What a married couple should save for their old age is each other.

Folks who saved for a rainy day are deluged by drips who didn't.

People who save pennies today probably tried dollars first.

When you finally save enough for a rainy day, your relatives start sending in bad weather reports.

TIME

Time is so powerful it is given to us only in small quantities.

Killing time is not murder, it's suicide.

Time may be a great healer, but it's no beauty specialist.

Daylight saving time just makes some people tired an hour earlier.

Tomorrow is often the busiest day of the year.

Time is what we want most, and what we use worst.

Today is yesterday shaking hands with tomorrow.

Time is the only money that can't be counterfeited.

When you kill time, just remember it has no resurrection.

Many people have time on their hands; also on their faces.

If you gave the same amount of time to your work as you do your church, how long would you hold your job?

Nothing makes time pass faster than vacations and short-term loans.

If you think time heals everything, try sitting it out in a doctor's office.

TOLERANCE

How to be tolerant: Learn to accept yourself, then you can accept anybody!

It is extremely difficult for the tolerant to tolerate the intolerant.

The test of courage comes when you are in the minority; the test of tolerance comes when you are in the majority.

Tolerance is that uncomfortable feeling that the other fellow may be right after all.

To permit others to be happy in their own way is tolerance at its highest level.

When some people yell for tolerance, what they really want is special privilege.

The average fellow seems to think more of tolerance than he does of truth.

Tolerance starts when you practice it; not when you just talk about it.

Proof that Americans are a tolerant people lies partly in the fact that the inventor of the juke box died a natural death.

126

Always be tolerant with a person who disagrees with you. After all, he has a right to his ridiculous opinions.

Perhaps the most impressive evidence of tolerance is a golden wedding anniversary.

Tolerance is the spirit of a man who knows—and who patiently listens to a fool who doesn't.

TONGUE (the)

If you must wag your tongue, always make it sound friendly.

A sharp tongue and a dull mind are usually found in the same head.

The human tongue is only a few inches from the brain, but when you listen to some people talk, they seem miles apart.

A bridle for the tongue is an excellent piece of harness.

Long tongues will mean short friends.

A sharp tongue is the only edge tool that grows keener with constant use.

Some people have eyes that see not and ears that hear not, but there are very few people who have tongues that talk not.

The tongue is a deadly weapon, whether it be sharp or blunt.

Cats are not the only ones that can lick themselves with their tongues.

Everybody agrees that a loose tongue can often lead to a few loose teeth.

The tongue was intended for a divine organ, but Satan often plays upon it.

A quiet tongue shows a wise head.

TROUBLE

Troubles are like babies, the more you nurse them the larger they grow.

If trouble was hard to get, people would gladly fight for it.

Trouble is usually produced by those who produce nothing else.

Nearly everybody has a remedy for the troubles of everybody except his own.

Never bear more than one kind of trouble at a time. Some people bear three: All they have now; all they have had; and all they expect to have.

Half our troubles come from wanting our own way. The other half comes from getting it.

Before you begin to tell your troubles to another person, ask yourself how you would like to listen to his.

You can't keep trouble from coming, but you needn't give it a chair to sit in.

Along with everything else, the facilities for getting into trouble have been improved.

Don't borrow trouble. Be patient and you'll soon have some of your own.

The fellow who is always telling us about his troubles is of some use—he keeps us from thinking about our own.

About the only thing you're sure to get by asking for it is trouble.

When you brood over your troubles you hatch despair.

Troubles in marriage often begin when a couple ceases to pitch woo and begins to throw fits.

People would have very little trouble if it weren't for other people.

You can always save yourself a lot of trouble by not borrowing any.

A good way to forget your troubles is to help others out of theirs.

Nowadays there is nothing brewing but trouble.

Much trouble is caused by our yearnings getting ahead of our earnings.

Most of us listen to the troubles of other people just for the chance to get back at them with our own.

If your troubles are deep-seated and long-standing, try kneeling.

The way some people go out of their way to look for trouble, you'd think trading stamps came with it.

One trouble with trouble is that it usually starts out like fun.

The only thing you can get in a hurry is trouble.

TRUTH

Not many people get weak eyes from searching for the truth.

Stretching may be an aid to health, but it doesn't seem to help the truth any.

We admire the truth, provided it agrees with our view.

The temple of truth has never suffered so much from woodpeckers on the outside as from termites from within.

Truth never dies, but it is often paralyzed by man's indifference.

The greatest homage you can pay the truth is to use it.

Truth is not only stranger than modern fiction, but is more decent.

The truth does not hurt unless it ought to.

Many people do not lie, they merely present the truth in such a way that nobody recognizes it.

Truth crushed to earth will rise again—but so will a lie.

The truth is one thing for which there are no known substitutes.

In this world, truth can wait; she's used to it.

Truth is so precious some people use it sparingly.

When truth stands in your way, it's time to change directions.

Truth is something which must be known with the mind, accepted with the heart, and enacted in life.

Two half truths do not necessarily constitute the whole truth.

It is seldom as hard to tell the truth as it is to hide it.

Truth fears nothing but concealment.

All truths are equally true but not equally important.

Some people stretch the truth; others mutilate it.

Let's all work together in an effort to stop truth decay.

Some people are just too modest to speak the naked truth.

Beware of the half truth. You might get hold of the wrong half.

Some agile people got that way from dodging the truth.

When you stretch the truth, watch out for the snap back.

U

UNBELIEF

Seeing ourselves as others see us wouldn't do much good, because most of us wouldn't believe what we saw.

UNITY

We cannot all play the same instrument, but we can all be in the same key.

V

VALUES

The most valuable thing a man can have up his sleeve is a good strong arm.

Don't buy it for a song—unless you're sure you know what the pitch is.

People who talk about the things they can't afford, sometimes forget that the list should include pride, envy, and malice.

It is unfortunate that so many citizens are demanding something for nothing. It is even more unfortunate that they are getting it.

We re-arrange our furniture, our flowers and our finances—but how about our values?

When we look at the price tag on some articles, we don't know whether they represent value or nerve.

The highest values cost no money and are priceless.

Some things cannot be measured. We do not think of a ton of truth, a bushel of beauty or an inspiration a mile long.

The things of greatest value in life are those things that multiply when divided.

Rejecting things because they are old-fashioned would rule out the sun, the moon, sunshine and rain—and a mother's love.

The value of all things, even our lives, depends on the use we make of them.

If this age is saved, it will be saved by the recovery of the sense of discrimination between what is passing and what is eternal.

Most folks pay too much for the things they get for nothing.

A sense of values is the most important single element in human personality.

VICES

Man's greatest vices are the misuse of his virtues.

Cultivate vices when you are young, and when you are old they will not forsake you.

All vices are of interior origin. Cards do not make the gambler nor a bottle the drunkard.

VIRTUE

Virtue has more admirers than followers.

If our good deeds were immediately and invariably rewarded, then virtue would become a racket.

Virtues are learned at mother's knee, and vices are learned at some other joint.

When one robs another of virtue he loses his own.

Rarely do we like the virtues we do not have.

Scientists claim nothing in the world can be destroyed. What about old-fashioned virtues?

While virtue is its own reward, most people are looking for a better offer.

W

WAGES

When you try to define a living wage, it depends on whether you are giving or getting it.

The trouble with take-home pay is that it won't stay there.

Wages can't meet high prices if they both are going in the same direction.

Increased earnings nearly always lead to increased yearnings.

Most folks need higher wages to pay the higher prices caused by higher wages.

You cannot lift the wage earner by pulling down the wage payer.

The wages of sin are about the only ones that are not being reduced.

It's easy to figure out a living wage for the other fellow to live on.

In the good old days the biggest grab for a man's salary took place after he got home.

The wages of sin are never frozen.

A living wage is a little more than you are now making.

WAR

The terrible thing about war is that it usually kills the wrong people.

War would be virtually impossible if everything were on a cash basis.

A great war leaves the country with three armies: An army of cripples, an army of widows, and an army of thieves.

The best way to end a war is not to begin it.

Modern war is like an argument with a woman—you can't win it or end it.

Will we ever see the last of war or will war see the last of us?

The greatest paradox of them all is to speak of "civilized" warfare.

Cold wars call for too much cold cash.

Every war is a national calamity whether victorious or not.

History reveals that wars create more problems than they solve.

Wars have a habit of coming when nations can least afford them.

Every cloud has a silver lining except a war cloud.

The nations of this world are so sick of war that to avoid it they are willing to do most anything except be reasonable.

About the only thing a war settles is a mortgage on the civilized world.

Evidently several other things must be banished before war is abolished.

In time of war, the first casualty is truth.

The war that will end war will not be fought with guns.

In an atomic war all men will be cremated equal.

War does not determine who is right—only who is left. Next time it won't do even that.

Older men declare war. But it is youth that must fight them.

There will be no more wars when nations learn how to completely bankrupt themselves without fighting.

Machinery and electricity now do most everything in wars—except the walking on crutches.

The tragedy of war is that it uses man's best to do man's worst.

In time of war the rich get the shekels and the poor get the shackles.

War does not, and never can, prove which side is right, but only which side is stronger.

WEALTH

Nothing distributes wealth like taxation and a large family.

There are two ways in which we may become wealthy: Spend less, and make more.

Wealth is a worry if you have it and a worry if you don't.

Untold wealth is the wealth which does not appear on income tax returns.

It is not wealth but the arrogance of wealth that offends the poor.

Wealth makes people admire in you qualities that you don't possess.

The real measure of a man's wealth is how much he would be worth if he lost all his money.

Among the many things a wealthy man finds coming his way are relatives.

Some people may still have their first dollar, but the man who is really wealthy is the fellow who still has his first friend.

Wealth may not bring happiness, but it seems to bring a pleasant kind of misery.

Most of us have two chances of becoming wealthy—slim and none.

Wealth is usually a curse—especially when the neighbors have it.

WILD OATS

Wild oats need no fertilizer.

If you want a sure crop and a big yield, sow wild oats.

The price of wheat rises and falls. The price of wild oats remains the same.

One thing about wild oats—sowing them is not confined to any one season of the year.

Wild oats take something out of the soil of a man's life that no system of crop rotation can restore.

This country would be better off if more parents stopped sowing wild oats and started cultivating their children.

Wild oats is a juvenile's favorite cereal.

WISDOM

If wisdom were on sale on the open market, the stupid wouldn't even ask the price.

There's no point in saving wisdom for a rainy day.

Wisdom is knowing when to speak your mind and when to mind your speech.

If you don't claim too much wisdom, people will give you credit for more than you have.

Wisdom is knowledge in action.

It takes a wise man to know when he is fighting for a principle, or merely defending a prejudice.

Many people might have attained to wisdom had they not assumed that they already had it.

To know what to do with what you know is the essence of true wisdom.

Most men wish they were as wise as they think their wives think they are.

A wise man will desire no more than he can get honestly, use wisely, and leave cheerfully.

Knowledge is knowing a fact. Wisdom is knowing what to do with that fact.

An unusual amount of common sense is sometimes called wisdom.

A wise man is not as certain of anything as a fool is of everything.

As a man grows older and wiser, he talks less and says more.

The worst thing about wisdom is that it can only be acquired on the installment plan.

True wisdom comes when we learn to discern the difference between the passing and the eternal in our lives.

Wisdom might be defined as having the means to make a fool of yourself and not doing it.

You can't pay cash for wisdom. It comes to you on the installment plan.

A wise man does FIRST what a fool does LAST.

WORDS

The four most important words in the English language are: I, me, mine and money.

It is vain to use words when deeds are expected.

Our words may hide our thoughts, but our actions will reveal them.

Words and feathers are easily scattered, but not easily gathered up.

One thing you can give and still keep is your word.

Right is a bigger word than either success or failure.

Those with the most to say usually say it with the fewest words.

Kind words can never die, but without kind deeds they would sound mighty sick.

Keep your words soft and sweet—you may have to eat them.

Many a blunt word has a sharp edge.

Words sometimes serve as a smokescreen to obscure the truth rather than as a searchlight to reveal it.

A spoken word and a thrown stone cannot be recalled.

WORK

About the only way work can kill a fellow is to scare him to death.

Hard work is the yeast that raises the dough.

Never buy anything with a handle on it. It means work.

Work isn't work if you like it.

Two things deprive people of their peace of mind: Work unfinished, and work not yet begun.

Men who dream of hitching their wagon to a star would be far better off to hitch up their pants and go to work.

The only folks who like hard work are those who are paying for it.

Work is a tonic that contains no habit-forming drugs.

Some people are so superstitious they won't work any week that has a Friday in it.

One blessing in being poor, honest and hard-working is that nobody envies you.

It will be a great day when everybody who has a job is working.

Hard work rarely kills because so few give it a chance.

One of the hardest ways to make a living is to work for it.

Work is the meat of life; pleasure, the dessert.

Almost any system will work if the people behind it will.

Nothing is hard work unless there is something else you'd rather be doing.

Some people are bent with work; others get crooked trying to avoid it.

Hard work doesn't hurt those who don't do any.

Some people are too heavy for light work, and others are too light for heavy work.

All things come to him who goes after what the other fellow waits for.

Do your work with a whole heart and you will succeed—there is so little competition.

Housework is something you do that nobody notices unless you don't do it.

Work hard. The job you save may be your own.

Some will give an honest day's work even if it takes them all week to do it.

It's simply fantastic the amount of work you can get done, if you don't do anything else.

There seems to be no cure for those who are allergic to work.

WORLD

The only thing wrong with the world is the people.

All the world lives in two tents: content and discontent.

The world at its worst needs the church at its best.

This isn't such a bad world after all—once you get used to being nervous about everything.

The world is composed of givers and takers. The takers may eat better, but the givers sleep better.

We can only change the world by changing men.

This world is somewhat like a fruit cake in that it would not be complete without a few nuts in it.

The world has too many cranks and not enough self-starters.

If it's such a small world, why does it cost so much to run it?

The world changes so fast that a man couldn't be wrong all the time even if he tried.

Wouldn't it be ironical if the world ended before man can destroy it?

The world is better either because you lived in it, or because you have left it.

What the world needs is an amplifier for the still, small voice.

The world would be immensely better off if people would do nothing when they have nothing to do.

If the creation of the world had been a federal project, it probably would have taken six years instead of six days.

The world isn't getting smaller—just some of the people who inhabit it.

If we wish to make a new world we have the material ready. The first one, too, was made out of chaos.

When the world starts making sense to you, it's time to see your psychiatrist.

Things are pretty well evened up in this world. Other people's troubles are not as bad as yours, but their children are a lot worse.

The world owes you a living, but only when you have earned it.

Maybe one of the things wrong with the world is that there are not enough leaders of men and too many chasers of women.

The trouble with the world is that so many people who stand up for their rights fall down miserably on their duties.

WORRY

Worry can't change the past, but it can ruin the present.

The fellow who never worries may not be smart enough to know what it's all about.

Youth isn't satisfied with a new deal—they want the whole deck.

It's a common mistake of youth to expect too much—too soon—for too little.

The young people of today are no worse than we were; they just have more ways of making fools of themselves.

One benefit of the present youth protests—it's stopped a lot of people from bragging about their kids.

Did you hear about the young fellow who spent two years trying to find himself? He got a hair cut and there he was!

We worry about the things we want to do but can't, in the place of doing that which we should—but don't.

People who like to worry have a greater and more varied number of things to choose from than ever before.

Anyone who doesn't worry about the world situation these days ought to have his television set examined.

Whenever you're robbed by worry, it is always an inside job.

Worry is like a rocking chair—it will give you something to do but it won't get you anywhere.

The reason worry kills more people than work is that people worry more than they work.

Worry is interest paid on trouble before it falls due.

Don't worry too much about what lies ahead. Go as far as you can see, and when you get there, you can see farther on.

The only person who can afford to worry is the one who doesn't need to.

There's not a worry in the world worth the worry.

People would worry less about what others think of them if they only realized how seldom they do.

Why worry about the future? The present is more than most of us can handle.

Worry never changes a single thing—except he who worries.

Things are really tough when you have so many worries that a new one has to be kept waiting until you can get around to it.

About the only way a fellow can keep from worrying these days is to keep his mind off his thoughts.

A good memory test: What did you worry about one year ago today?

To worry about what we can't help is useless; to worry about what we can help is stupid.

Those who live in a worry invite death in a hurry.

All the worry you can have is what you carry around under your hat.

"Don't worry" is a better motto if you add the word, "others."

Perpetual worry will get you to one place ahead of time—the cemetery.

Don't worry about the job you don't like. Some one else will soon have it.

WORSHIP

Satan doesn't care what we worship, so long as we don't worship God.

Too many try to get something from worship without putting something into it.

A place of worship should be of such character that it will be easy for men to find God and difficult for them to forget Him.

If we are going to fight for the liberty to worship, we ought to make use of that liberty.

Y

YOUTH

The typical American youth is always ready to give those who are older than himself the full benefit of his inexperience.

Getting the baby to sleep is hardest when she is eighteen years old.

A mis-spent youth may result in a tragic old age.

The younger generation knows more than the old folks about everything except making a living.

Probably the most powerful head of steam ever created is that of young people trying to set on fire a world that is all wet.

The young people of today are tomorrow's leaders, but we sometimes wonder whether they are going to be followed or chased.

A great many young men are like Easter hats—mostly trimmings.

Young man, don't keep telling your best girl friend that you are unworthy of her. Let it be a surprise.

The main trouble with the youth movement is that it is getting too far away from the woodshed.

People who wonder where this generation is headed will do well to consider where it came from.

Two good openings for a young man are the legs in a pair of overalls.

A youth with his first cigar makes himself sick; a youth with his first girl friend makes other people sick.

About the only way to stay young is to live honestly, eat sensibly, sleep well, work hard, worship regularly, and lie about your age.

Youth is like fashion. Both fade quickly.

Young men should not get groggy over girls, religion, words, or politics. They are all good in moderation, but bad if they get an over-dose.

Z

ZEAL

Zeal is for the wise, but it is found mostly in fools.

If people were more zealous and less jealous, this world would be a better place in which to live.

Zeal without knowledge is the sister of folly.

There is no zeal so intemperate and cruel as that which is backed by ignorance.

Zeal without tolerance is fanaticism.